xx(1

LEGITIMATE EXPECTATIONS AND PROPORTIONALITY IN ADMINISTRATIVE LAW

Legitimate Expectations and Proportionality in Administrative Law

by

ROBERT THOMAS LLB, Ph.D

University of Manchester

·HART·
PUBLISHING

OXFORD – PORTLAND OREGON

2000

Hart Publishing
Oxford and Portland, Oregon

Published in North America (US and Canada) by
Hart Publishing c/o
International Specialized Book Services
5804 NE Hassalo Street
Portland, Oregon
97213-3644
USA

Distributed in the Netherlands, Belgium and Luxembourg by
Intersentia, Churchillaan 108
B2900 Schoten
Antwerpen
Belgium

Hart Publishing Ltd is a specialist legal publisher based in Oxford, England.
To order further copies of this book or to request a list of other
publications please write to:

Hart Publishing Ltd, Salter's Boatyard, Oxford OX1 4LB
Telephone: +44 (0)1865 245533 or Fax: +44 (0)1865 794882
e-mail: mail@hartpub.co.uk
www.hartpub.co.uk

British Library Cataloguing in Publication Data
Data Available
ISBN 1 84113-086-9 (cloth)

Typeset by Hope Services (Abingdon) Ltd.
Printed in Great Britain on acid-free paper
by Biddles Ltd, Guildford and King's Lynn.

Preface

This book is a revised version of a doctoral thesis submitted to the University of Nottingham in 1998. My purpose in this book is to assess how the English courts have responded to two legal principles, legitimate expectations and proportionality, which originally developed in German law but which have been made more prominent through European Community law. This assessment is conducted by way of a comparison of the case law of the English courts and the European Court of Justice. While this book is primarily aimed at English public lawyers, I hope it will be of interest to lawyers from other jurisdictions interested in judicial review of administrative action.

My interest in the development of legitimate expectations and proportionality was aroused by the need to understand why these two principles should present such apparent difficulties for English law when they are readily accepted in European Community law. As my research progressed I came to recognise that the difficulties did not stem from the innate nature of the principles themselves. Rather, the problems associated with them were intimately connected with the different cultural approaches to the appropriate place and role of law in the modern state between England and the Continent. Furthermore, this suggested that if there was to be any reconciliation of the principles in English law, then it would require a reconsideration of the basic conception of administrative legality. If anything, therefore, I hope that this book contributes to the general debate concerning the appropriate role of law in government.

In writing this book I have incurred many debts and would like to express my thanks to various people. I am particularly grateful to Alastair Mowbray and Stephen Weatherill who, as my supervisors at Nottingham University, provided me with the encouragement, support and guidance necessary to complete the thesis. I am indebted to the Department of Law at Nottingham for its generous financial assistance. Antony Arnull and Sue Arrowsmith subjected the thesis to a thorough examination; I am very grateful to them. I would like to thank Sir William Wade for answering my inquiries regarding Lord Diplock. I would also like to thank John Bell, Nicola Glover, Tim Jones, Martin Loughlin and Thomas Poole for commenting on various drafts when I was in the process of revising the thesis for publication. Finally, I would like to express my gratitude to my friends and family who supported me even though they did not always understand what I was trying to do. Most of all, however, I need to thank Nicola who has always encouraged and supported me and tolerated the more stressful moments involved in writing this book.

Robert Thomas
January 2000

Contents

Table of Cases

EUROPEAN COURT OF JUSTICE

Germany

Introduction

Legitimate expectations and proportionality are legal principles which inform and control the implementation of public policy by administrative authorities. Both principles originally developed in German public law. During the 1970s and 1980s they began to gain an acceptance in European Community law and English law. Since then, legitimate expectations and proportionality have, on the whole, come to be accepted as general principles of administrative law. The purpose of this book is to evaluate the integration of the principles into English law by comparing the case law of the English courts with that of the European Court of Justice.

Legitimate expectations means that any individual who, as a result of governmental conduct, holds certain expectations concerning future governmental activity, can require those expectations to be fulfilled unless there are compelling public interest reasons for not doing so. Proportionality means that a public authority should adopt only those measures which are strictly necessary for the performance of its functions. If the public authority has a choice between several appropriate measures then recourse should be made to the mildest and least-restrictive course of action available. As Lord Diplock once put it, "'You must not use a steam hammer to crack a nut, if a nutcracker would do'".[1]

There has been plenty of scholarly examination of the principles in European Community law and English law. However, to my knowledge no one has attempted to evaluate and compare the case law of the English courts with that of the European Court of Justice. I believe that such a comparison could provide an illuminating way of examining how the English courts have sought to integrate the principles into English law. After all, if we wish to evaluate the integration of the principles in English law then we need a standard of comparison. As the European Court of Justice introduced legitimate expectations and proportionality over the same period of time as the English courts, its jurisprudence may be used for the purposes of comparison. A second reason for using European Community law arises from the duty on English courts to apply these and other principles when enforcing Community law. In light of this it would be relevant to examine whether the application of the principles as a matter of Community law has had any influence on domestic law.

An inquiry concerning the integration of the principles also raises a much wider theme; namely, the appropriate role of law in government. How should the law respond to the exercise of administrative power? Debates and arguments over the application of legitimate expectations and proportionality reflect

---

[1] *R. v. Goldstein* [1983] 1 All ER 434, 436e.

wider concerns of how the law should intervene in public administration. In this regard there is a notable difference of approach between Continental Europe and England. In the legal systems of Continental states administrative law typically forms a distinct form of legal inquiry, with administrative courts applying special public law principles to regulate state activity. By contrast, in England the common law has traditionally emphasised the universality of the law and rejected the need for separate legal consideration of issues arising from the growth of governmental activity. Principles drawn from French and German law have also influenced European Community law. It is therefore important to pay regard to the different approaches to administrative law between England and Continental Europe when comparing the development of legitimate expectations and proportionality.

However, while such traditions form the basis from which any examination of the principles must begin, they do not determine the appropriate role of law in the future. For example, in England there is considerable disagreement concerning the role of law in government. In this book I will attempt to contribute to this debate by suggesting the approach English courts should adopt if they are to integrate legitimate expectations and proportionality into English law.

Therefore, my objective in this book is to examine and compare the integration of legitimate expectations and proportionality in English law with their elaboration in European Community law. In doing so it is imperative to bring to light the different attitudes towards the role of law in government. This is the subject of chapter 1. Chapter 2 examines why the two principles have come to gain acceptance in English law. The following three chapters are concerned with the comparison of the principles in English and European Community law. Legitimate expectations is dealt with in chapter 3. The examination of proportionality is divided between two chapters: chapter 4 focuses upon proportionality in European Community law and the debate among English lawyers concerning its possible adoption; chapter 5 asks how this principle could be integrated into English law and what changes are necessary for that end. I conclude by considering how the English courts have fared and how they could integrate the principles more effectively.

1

Approaches to Administrative Law

THE GROWTH OF administrative power over the last century and more has presented a major challenge for the legal systems of most developed countries. The modern administrative state undertakes tasks and manages programmes on an unprecedented scale in order to satisfy the needs of the complex societies in which we live. Much political debate is concerned with the extent and reach of the state, whether it ought to pursue certain objectives and, if so, whether it can do so successfully. However, as the range of tasks performed by the administration has increased, so has the potential for arbitrary or unfair action as regards the individual. The nature of the challenge for the legal system has been to recognise that while administrators perform legitimate social functions, they also exercise powers which may adversely affect the interests of the individual citizen and therefore need to be subject to legal supervision. The response of different legal cultures to this challenge has varied. In Continental European states it was generally recognised that a separate law of public administration was needed to control and supervise the activities of the state. Courts of public administration were established which developed distinct principles of public law, such as legitimate expectations and proportionality, in order to strike a fair balance between the exercise of public functions and the protection of private interests. By contrast, in England the growth of public administration was accommodated within the established traditions of the common law as evolved by the ordinary courts. Public authorities were subject to the same legal processes and principles as those which applied between private individuals. The last few decades have seen a distinct change of attitude as the English courts have begun to draw a conceptual distinction between public and private law proceedings. The principles of legitimate expectations and proportionality, which provide the primary focus here, have been increasingly employed by English judges wishing to ensure that administrators show proper respect for individuals. However, while in other legal orders public law principles have evolved hand in hand with the existence of a separate system of administrative law, the English courts have struggled to elaborate distinct principles from within the common law tradition; and that struggle is the subject of this book.

This chapter addresses the development of administrative law in both England and Europe. Its purpose is to identify the cultural orientations towards administrative law which exist within the institutional structures of the legal systems. The aim here is to explicate the differences of approach between the common law and the legal systems of Continental states such as France and Germany. Confusion and misunderstanding may be avoided if it is possible to appreciate that "administrative law" in England means something quite different from either *droit administratif* or *verwaltungsrecht*. As both French and German law have exerted a powerful influence on the development of administrative law in the European Community, it is necessary to have regard to such legal traditions in order to appreciate the jurisprudence of the European Court of Justice. In particular, this chapter will highlight how such states have used the law constructively as a means of controlling and guiding the state; whereas in England we have, on the whole, been unable to achieve a comparable disposition. Furthermore, the debates concerning the principles of legitimate expectations and proportionality have been informed by established traditions of public law thought. In order to understand these debates it is therefore necessary to discern the distinctiveness of such thought. Indeed, this task of making explicit the different orientations towards the role of law in public administration is essential if we are to understand and compare the development of legitimate expectations and proportionality in English and European law. Before doing so, however, it is necessary to address the issue of how administrative power has grown, and the general meaning attributed to "administrative law".

The organisation of public administration is a product of cultural, political and historical forces that impact upon the national state. Structures of governance are inseparable from their political context. Similarly, administrative law has long been viewed as an area of law directly connected with the national organisation of the state and therefore incapable of rendering generalisation applicable to all states.[1] However, for several decades two developments have impacted upon administrative organisation in Europe: the expansion of the state and European integration through the European Union. The increase in the complexity of modern societies has led to a greater role for the intervention of the state and a huge increase in law-making. A functionally specialised class of administrators grew in number in order to realise the attainment of social purposes. This, in turn, resulted in an explosion in the making of positive law in light of the demands placed upon government. Such laws are highly specific, differentiated and variable rules of public administration. Administrative law in this sense is an instrument of social change and a mechanism for distributing opportunities created by social development. It is validated by reason of a political decision to pursue a policy of social improvement. Furthermore, as European states pursue common objectives through the European Union, positive law-making extends to the supranational level as demonstrated by the constant stream of regulations, directives and decisions flowing from the European institutions.

---

[1] See, e.g., U. Scheuner, "*Der Einfluß des französischen Verwaltungsrechts auf die deutsche Rechtsentwicklung*" (1963) 16 *Die Öffentliche Verwaltung* 714; O. Kahn-Freund, "On Uses and Misuses of Comparative Law" (1974) 37 *MLR* 1, 17.

Another conception of "administrative law" concerns the legal principles of government. Administrative law in this sense provides the principles and rules which control and regulate the administrative state in its dealings with the individual. The courts enforce norms of legality to ensure that government respects the rule of law. This is the more commonly used meaning of the term, with the focus upon judicial review of administrative action. In this sense administrative law does not originate from the administration but from the courts. However, administrators pursue collective goals as selected through the process of democratic will-formation and made legally binding through positive law. If the courts are to lay down the standards against which governmental action is to be tested, then, in doing so, should they have regard to the objectives of administration? To understand the responses to this issue it is necessary to examine the different legal traditions.

ADMINISTRATIVE LAW IN ENGLAND

The traditional account of English public law is well known.[2] Its defining features have been that Parliament is sovereign and that the rule of law requires all individuals and public bodies to be subject to the ordinary law of the land. Public authorities are not entitled to be treated any differently than private individuals, and the exercise of public power is to be channelled through Parliament. While this traditional account was a product of Victorian England, it also became the dominant approach to law and the constitution in the twentieth century. A distinctive characteristic of this has been the value placed upon conventions and established practices of British government. Such practices have ensured a sense of continuity between past and present in order to accommodate new developments. The dominant political culture has relied heavily on the practical experience of the governing class who, having been educated with its traditions, knew how to operate the "dignified" and "efficient" parts of the constitution.[3] Although Parliament was omnipotent there was little danger of any abuse of power because of the prudent self-limitation of its members. In contrast with Continental states with bureaucratic structures, Britain was governed through the informal networks and processes of "club government", with public administration seen more as of a form of art than a distinct science. Michael Oakeshott captured the distinctiveness of this style when he argued that politics arises not from a rational selection of specific objectives but from a tradition of behaviour:[4]

---

[2] A.V. Dicey, *An Introduction to the Study of the Law of the Constitution* [1885] (Macmillan, London, 10th ed. 1959).

[3] W. Bagehot, *The English Constitution* [1867] (Fontana, London, 1993), 63.

[4] M. Oakeshott, *Rationalism in Politics and other essays* (Methuen, London, 1962), 127.

"[i]n political activity . . . men sail a boundless and bottomless sea; there is neither harbour for shelter nor floor for anchorage, neither starting-place nor appointed destination. The enterprise is to keep afloat on an even keel."

In relation to law, such traditions have been reflected in common law, with its reliance upon the practical experience of judges. The common law is not an exact science, but more the product of the good wisdom of its judges. As Sir Edward Coke C.J. famously intoned, law is the "artificial perfection of Reason gotten by long Study, Observation and Experience".[5] In contrast with Continental legal systems, Roman law was never influential in England. Its rational and systematic style could not penetrate the "common law mind" associated with the myth of the ancient constitution.[6] Instead, law was seen as the result of immemorial custom and the accumulated wisdom of judicial experience. In this way the common law came to be seen as having the advantage of both continuity and innovation as it was capable of being up to date, whilst having existed "time out of mind of man".[7] Underpinning this heritage of political tradition and the common law is an anti-rationalist style of thought, which places importance on the practical experience of its participants, established traditions and customs. Constitutional conventions and the common law are products of such practical knowledge and are not capable of precise formulation; they can only be acquired or imparted through practice.[8] The dominance of this style of thought can clearly be seen underlying the common law method in which judges use precedents to decide cases through the artificial reason of law. It was against this background that A.V. Dicey, being "the first to apply the analytical method to English public law",[9] formulated the principles of the law of the constitution. For Dicey, Parliamentary sovereignty was an undoubted legal fact and the rule of law required the application of the regular law by the ordinary courts as opposed to the arbitrary power exercised by government.

One upshot of this cultural heritage has been that English lawyers have not been required to develop a legal conception of the state relevant to modern government. England lacks a tradition of viewing the state as a distinct legal entity.[10] There is no concept equivalent to the French *l'état de droit* or the German *Rechtsstaat*. Instead, the confused concept of the Crown or sovereignty of Parliament has been used to explain the exercise of public power. In the absence of a decisive break in the political regime, Britain has experienced an unusual degree of continuity in its institutions and traditions. Despite the vast changes in the size and scale of governmental activity and the gradual extension

[5] Coke 1 *Institutes*, section 138. See also *Prohibitions del Roy* (1607) 12 *Co. Rep.* 63.
[6] See J.G.A. Pocock, *The Ancient Constitution and the Feudal Law: A Study of English Historical Thought in the Seventeenth Century* (Cambridge University Press, Cambridge, revised ed. 1987), ch. 2.
[7] Sir Edward Coke C.J., *The Third Part of the Reports of Edward Coke* (revised ed. 1738), vii.
[8] Oakeshott, above at n. 4.
[9] W.I. Jennings, *The Law and the Constitution* (London University Press, London, 1933), x.
[10] K.H.F. Dyson, *The State Tradition in Western Europe: A Study of an Idea and Institution* (Martin Robertson, Oxford, 1980), viii, 36–44.

of democratic politics, the institutional and cultural heritage has largely remained the same. The comment of the German comparativist, Josef Redlich, that Victorian England lacked an abstract theory of the state and its jurisprudence was unequipped with a theory of administration could equally be applied to modern day England.[11] Rather than re-conceptualising the role of law in response to the changing relationship between the individual and the state, the dominant tradition of public law preferred to accommodate such developments within established arrangements. The emergence of a more rational and ideological form of politics within this anti-rationalist constitutional framework has inevitably caused strains. For traditionalists, such as Lord Hailsham, such tensions have resulted in the displacement of the old practices with an "elective dictatorship" of the executive in Parliament.[12] However, others have argued that Britain has failed to develop a constitution appropriate to contemporary needs and demands.[13]

The common law has also encountered various pressures to respond to the growth in governmental activity. When Dicey, in 1885, declared the rule of law to be a marked feature of the constitution he was, in effect, celebrating the limited role of government in the polity. Dicey opposed collectivist or social legislation because it weakened the moral fibre of the people: "State help kills self-help".[14] The definition that Dicey gave to the rule of law was predicated upon these assumptions. Rather than being subject to special legal controls, disputes between public authorities and individuals were decided by recourse to ordinary private law principles. According to Dicey, the existence of a separate system of administrative law, such as in Continental states, particularly France, rested on "ideas foreign to the fundamental assumptions of our English common law, and especially . . . the rule of law".[15] A separate administrative law would undermine the universality of the law and place the state in a privileged position. By contrast, the common law did not allow public authorities to "shelter behind a *droit administratif*".[16] For Dicey there was a fundamental incompatibility between the regular law and existence of arbitrary governmental power. A separate administrative law was viewed as a means of enshrining arbitrariness rather than reflecting basic developments in social functions expressed through the growth of the state. The dependence of Dicey's constitutionalism upon the assumption of limited government and a negative conception of liberty

[11] J. Redlich and F.W. Hirst, *Local Government in England* (Macmillan, London, 1903), 376–7.

[12] Lord Hailsham, *The Dilemma of Democracy: Diagnosis and Prescription* (Collins, London, 1978), ch. xx.

[13] See, e.g., D. Marquand, *The Unprincipled Society: New Demands and Old Politics* (Jonathan Cape, London, 1988), ch. 7; W. Hutton, *The State We're In* (Vintage, London, new ed. 1996), ch. 11.

[14] A.V. Dicey, *Lectures on the Relationship Between Law and Public Opinion in England during the Nineteenth Century* (Macmillan, London, 1905), 256.

[15] Dicey, above at n. 2, 329. See R. Errera, "Dicey and French Administrative Law: A Missed Encounter?" [1985] PL 695.

[16] *Ministry of Housing and Local Government* v. *Sharp* [1970] 2 QB 223, 266D, *per* Lord Denning M.R., and 275B, *per* Salmon L.J. See also *In re Grosvenor Hotel, London (No. 2)* [1965] Ch. 1210, 1261, *per* Salmon L.J.

is illustrated by his change of opinion concerning the rule of law. In 1885 Dicey had proudly declared the rule of law to be a special attribute of the common law. However, only thirty years later, during a period of huge social and political change his celebratory rhetoric was replaced with an almost despairing attitude towards the growth of the state. Dicey noted that the "ancient veneration for the rule of law has in England suffered . . . a marked decline".[17] The extended franchise had led to the increased use of legislation for social ends which, in Dicey's opinion, diminished respect for the rule of law and upset the balance of the polity. However, regardless of his change of view, Dicey's work enjoyed huge success largely because he was able, as a "public moralist", to address the concerns of a conservative-minded legal profession.[18]

While basic social and political changes were occurring, the imprint that Dicey made upon our understanding of law and the constitution proved sufficiently deep to prevent a re-conceptualisation of the relationship between law and administration. As the growth in the scale and complexity of the state was achieved by a vast increase in legislation, statutes came to displace the common law as the basic source of law. However, a corresponding change did not take place at the level of the conception of legality. The dominant view of law has remained at the level of common law thought, despite the development and growth of state functions. The result has been that law is viewed merely as a means of controlling the exercise of public power and not as a means of facilitating or structuring administrative action. Dicey's legacy was to preclude the development of a separate administrative law that was not contrary to the definition he had given to the rule of law. Unable to prevent the growth in government, the influence exerted by Dicey's theory was to obfuscate these issues and prevent the rationalisation of constitutional arrangements in light of such changes. Dicey's success was to develop a style that enabled the anti-rationalist culture of the common law and an individualist conception of the state to become established as the dominant tradition of public law through a positivist analysis of law. Furthermore, as most public lawyers have continued to work within this style of analytical jurisprudence, this has exercised a profound influence in bolstering the traditional orthodoxy. The upshot of all this was that both professional and academic public lawyers became peripheral actors in the face of the developments in the scale and complexity of state activity.

However, not every lawyer agreed with either Dicey's views or his approach. During the inter-war period some writers applied a functionalist approach to the role of law in public administration and sought constructively to meet the challenges for law presented by the growth of administrative power. William

---

[17] A.V. Dicey, *An Introduction to the Study of the Law of the Constitution* (Macmillan, London, 8th ed. 1915), xxxviii. In the 1915 edition of his work, Dicey added a lengthy introduction in which he compared the constitution of 1885 with that of 1914.

[18] See S. Collini, *Public Moralists: Political Thought and Intellectual Life in Britain 1850–1930* (Clarendon Press, Oxford, 1991), 287–301.

Robson's work, *Justice and Administrative Law*,[19] was written in order to dispel the illusion that there was no administrative law in Britain.[20] Robson argued that merely because there was no equivalent to *droit administratif* in England, it did not follow that there was no system of administrative law. The extension of governmental activities had increased the importance of administration and resulted in a vast body of administrative law. For Robson this comprised of the law relating to public administration and was inherently connected with social development. The problem was not to discover its existence, but to "master its widespread ramifications and to reduce it to some kind of order and coherence".[21] To achieve this Robson argued that the haphazard arrangements had to be rationalised into a system of public law. Sir Ivor Jennings argued that Dicey's writings could only be understood against his Whig individualism[22] and sought to redefine the role of the lawyer in view of the growth of administrative power:[23]

> "The task of the lawyer as such is not to declare that modern intervention is pernicious, but, seeing that all modern States have adopted the policy, to advise as to the technical devices which are necessary to make the policy efficient and to provide justice for individuals."

These public lawyers argued that the growth of administrative discretion required new ideas and new institutions rather than disapproval of the extension of government combined with complacent nostalgia for past constitutional arrangements.[24] Both Robson and Jennings argued for the establishment of a Continental style administrative court to hear appeals from administrative tribunals.[25] To resolve disputes concerning the application of policy, it was argued that such an appellate body should be separate from the traditions of the common law as they were incompatible with the philosophy underlying social legislation, and be staffed by those with knowledge and experience of public administration. However, the Committee on Ministers' Powers rejected the idea of a separate administrative jurisdiction.[26] Since the terms of reference for the Committee were to "report what safeguards are desirable or necessary to secure the constitutional principles of the sovereignty of Parliament and the supremacy of the Law",[27] its recommendations did not come as a complete surprise. In

---

[19] W.A. Robson, *Justice and Administrative Law: A Study of the British Constitution* (Stevens, London, 3rd ed. 1951).

[20] W.A. Robson, "Justice and Administrative Law Reconsidered" (1979) 32 *CLP* 107.

[21] Robson, above at n. 19, 32.

[22] W.I. Jennings, "In Praise of Dicey 1885–1935" (1935) 13 *Public Administration* 123, 124–33.

[23] W.I. Jennings, "Courts and Administrative Law—The Experience of English Housing Law Legislation" (1936) 49 *Harvard LR* 426, 430.

[24] See W.A. Robson, *Public Administration Today* (Stevens, London, 1948), 15–17.

[25] Robson, above at n. 19, 426–9; W.I. Jennings "The Report on Ministers' Powers" (1932) 10 *Public Administration* 333, 348–51; J. Willis, *The Parliamentary Powers of Government Departments* (Cambridge University Press, Cambridge, 1933), 172.

[26] *The Report of the Committee on Ministers' Powers Report*, Cmd 4060 (HMSO, London, 1932).

[27] Ibid., section 1, para. 1.

Robson's opinion the Committee had "started life with the dead hand of Dicey lying frozen on its neck".[28] In the post-war period the functionalist style was exemplified by J.D.B. Mitchell, who argued that English public law remained underdeveloped because of the dominant legal culture. Excessive reliance upon the two dogmas of Parliamentary sovereignty and control by the ordinary courts prevented the creation of an administrative law with appropriate machinery to meet new challenges. Mitchell considered that the problem for public law was that it was "too often regarded as a series of unfortunate exceptions to the desirable generality or universality of the rules of private law, and . . . [was] . . . not seen as a rational system with its own justification, and perhaps its own philosophy".[29] However, while the functionalist style of thought provided valuable critiques of the dominant legal culture it was never able to displace it.

In light of the absence of a separate administrative jurisdiction it fell to the ordinary courts to fill the gap. While the courts would sometimes exercise restraint when faced with challenges to the use of administrative power, on other occasions they would seem to go out of their way to prevent public author- ities from achieving their chosen purposes.[30] From a traditionalist perspective Lord Hewart fulminated against the growth of "administrative lawlessness" which was undermining the rule of law.[31] From a functionalist perspective, it was argued that the courts' decisions displayed a distrust of administrative power. Not only did courts lack the institutional ability to resolve new issues coming before them, but their judgments also reflected a preference for private rights rather than public duties.[32] Following the formation of the welfare state the issue became impossible to ignore. For instance, a reviewer of C.J. Hamson's Hamlyn lectures on the *Conseil d'État* could sympathise with the embarrassment of comparing the French system of administrative justice with the English common law; the latter was "living in a state of decayed gentility".[33] Members of the judiciary expressed different views. While Lord Denning was convinced of the need to modernise the machinery of securing remedies from the state,[34] others expressed a more pessimistic view. Lord Devlin considered that the common law "no longer . . . [had] . . . the strength to provide any satisfac-

---

[28] Robson, above at n. 19, 423.

[29] J.D.B. Mitchell, "The Causes and Effects of the Absence of a System of Public Law in the United Kingdom" [1965] *PL* 94, 95.

[30] Compare *Local Government Board* v. *Arlidge* [1915] AC 120, with *Roberts* v. *Hopwood* [1925] AC 578.

[31] Lord Hewart of Bury, *The New Despotism* (Benn, London, 1929), 13. See also C.K. Allen, *Law in the Making* (London, 1927); C.K. Allen, *Bureaucracy Triumphant* (London, 1931).

[32] See, e.g., H.J. Laski, "Judicial Review of Social Policy in England" (1926) 39 *Harvard LR* 832; J. Willis, "Three Approaches to Administrative Law: the Judicial, the Conceptual and the Functional" (1935) 1 *University of Toronto LJ* 53; Jennings, above at n. 23; Robson, above at n. 19.

[33] F.H. Newark, Book Review (1955) 71 *LQR* 571. Cf C.J. Hamson, *Executive Discretion and Judicial Control: An Aspect of the French Conseil d'État* (Stevens, London, 1954).

[34] A. Denning, *Freedom Under the Law* (Stevens, London, 1949), chs 3 and 4. See also H.W.R. Wade, "Law, Opinion and Administration" (1962) 78 *LQR* 188.

tory solution to the problem of keeping the executive . . . under proper control".[35] Despite these early disagreements, the courts gradually became more willing to referee disputes between individuals and public authorities. In a process marked by fits and starts the courts sought to rediscover "their historic but long-neglected role as protectors of the private citizen against unlawful or unjust treatment by the executive".[36]

The principal features of this project, such as the resurrection of the old prerogative writs and the removal of obstacles to the control of administrative power, are well known. The revival of principles and remedies is undeniable.[37] However, this development has taken place within the terms of the traditional account of public law and the culture of common law. While administrative law is no longer considered to be "fundamentally inconsistent" with the rule of law, the values and beliefs articulated by Dicey can still be found in leading textbooks and court judgments.[38] The judges have articulated a traditional model of judicial review in which it is their role to enforce the intention of Parliament, supplemented by their customary wisdom, as the guardians of common law. Within this conception of judicial review, the principal tool used by the judiciary is the *ultra vires* rule to ensure that public authorities do not act outside their jurisdiction. Natural justice ensures fair procedures, and unreasonableness allows judges to filter out objectionable decisions. A model of public law has been developed through the interstices of private law. Consequently, as the distinctiveness of public law is generally not acknowledged, this traditional model of judicial review has lacked a coherent justification and consistent principles.[39] While the British state has experienced the socialisation of government, its legal culture has failed to provide an adequate and constructive response to the socialisation of law because of the assumption of a strict division between law and government which is deeply rooted in legal thought.

In light of social, economic and technological developments, various public lawyers have perceived the limitations of the traditional conception of public law. Their principal concerns have been that the traditional model provides an insufficiently secure protection of the individual against the state and an inadequately theorised public law. Instead of working within the confines of the traditional model, some writers have sought to replace it with a liberal conception of public law. The objective of this liberal style of thought is to construct a rational and principled public law which emphasises the importance of protecting individual freedom against intrusion by the state. In arguing that the foundations

---

[35] P. Devlin, "The Common Law, Public Policy and the Executive" (1956) 9 *CLP* 1, 14. See also G.W. Keeton, "The Twilight of the Common Law" (1949) *The Nineteenth Century and After* 230.

[36] Lord Diplock, "Administrative Law: Judicial Review Reviewed" (1974) 33 *CLJ* 233.

[37] For an account of this see J.M. Jacob, *The Republican Crown: Lawyers and the Making of the State in Twentieth Century Britain* (Dartmouth, Aldershot, 1996).

[38] See, e.g., H.W.R. Wade and C.F. Forsyth, *Administrative Law* (Clarendon Press, Oxford, 7th ed. 1994).

[39] See, e.g., Lord Scarman, "The Development of Administrative Law: Obstacles and Opportunities" [1990] *PL* 490.

of judicial review are no longer found in jurisdiction but in a substantive conception of the rule of law, such writers have sought to re-focus public law on the protection of individual rights through the elaboration of principled judicial justification. Inspired by Ronald Dworkin's theory of rights[40] and F.A. Hayek's liberal constitutionalism,[41] writers such as Jeffrey Jowell and Anthony Lester,[42] and T.R.S. Allan[43] have urged the courts to use rational principles, in particular the principle of proportionality, to protect the individual against the state. These "liberal constitutionalists" have argued for principles to restrain the state because the traditional approach is no longer considered capable of imposing clear limits on state activity in light of the increasing complexity of modern governance.[44] The informal networks of club government can be manipulated in order to evade accountability and therefore greater legal controls of government are necessary. However, the argument of the liberal constitutionalists extends beyond critique; it also contains a strong normative dimension. They argue that the British constitution is predicated upon a liberal conception of the relationship between individual and the state. An important feature of this project is therefore its orientation towards more rational principles of judicial review as opposed to the anti-rationalist tendencies of the traditional approach. Significantly, the project has received support from some members of the judiciary. For instance, Sir John Laws has been particularly vocal in arguing for the High Court to act as the guardian of fundamental constitutional rights, that the rule of law is a moral requirement demanded by the autonomy of individuals and that the foundations of public law are to be found in the shared morality of the community.[45]

While liberal constitutionalists seek new rational principles to replace the customary wisdom of judges, their style of thought shares with the traditional model a need to ground law in some normative, non-purposive basis. Law is viewed as necessarily prior to both government and legislation and as a means of preventing government from overstepping its proper limits. Both traditional

---

[40] R. Dworkin, *Taking Rights Seriously* (Duckworth, London, 1977); R. Dworkin, *Law's Empire* (Fontana, London, 1986).

[41] F.A. Hayek, *The Constitution of Liberty* (Routledge, London, 1960); F.A. Hayek, *Law, Legislation and Liberty: A new statement of the liberal principles of justice and political economy. Volume 1: Rules and Order* (Routledge, London, 1973), *Volume 2: The Mirage of Social Justice* (Routledge, London, 1976), *Volume 3: The Political Order of a Free People* (Routledge, London, 1979).

[42] J. Jowell and A. Lester, "Beyond *Wednesbury*: Substantive Principles of Administrative Law" [1987] *PL* 368; J. Jowell, "Restraining the State: Politics, Principle and Judicial Review" (1997) 50 *CLP* 189 (special edition entitled *Law and Opinion at the end of Twentieth Century*).

[43] T.R.S. Allan, *Law, Liberty, and Justice: The Legal Foundations of British Constitutionalism* (Clarendon Press, Oxford, 1993).

[44] M. Loughlin, *Public Law and Political Theory* (Clarendon Press, Oxford, 1992), uses the phrase "liberal normativists".

[45] Sir John Laws, "Is the High Court the Guardian of Fundamental Constitutional Rights?" [1993] *PL* 59; Sir John Laws, "The Constitution: Morals and Rights" [1996] *PL* 622; Sir John Laws, "The Constitutional Foundations of Modern Public Law" (1998) 10 *European Review of Public Law* 579.

and liberal modes of thought are therefore in contrast with the functionalist style in which law is seen as a necessary feature of government in an increasingly complex society and which focuses upon the ability of law to contribute towards the attainment of public purposes. These distinct strands of public law thought have been discussed for two reasons: first, they demonstrate the lack of consensus concerning the most basic issues of public law; and, secondly, contemporary judicial review is relatively fluid and judges tend to change from a traditional model of judicial review to a more liberal or rights-based approach from case to case without providing any clear explanation why a different perspective is being adopted. While the traditional model of public law has historically provided the dominant approach to the subject, this style of thought has, in recent years, been experiencing a dissipation of its authority in favour of a more rationalistic and liberal-oriented conception of public law.

ADMINISTRATIVE LAW IN EUROPE

Continental conceptions of administrative law, in particular French and German law, have exerted a pervasive influence over the development of the administrative law of the European Community.[46] In order to define the rules of law relating to the application of the EC Treaty, the European Court of Justice has utilised a comparative method in order to draw upon the laws of domestic legal systems.[47] In doing so the Court has not been content to adopt those principles which are merely "arithmetical 'common denominators'" between the legal systems of the Member States but has chosen those which it considers to be the most "progressive" or "carefully considered" having regard to the objects of the Treaty.[48] Continental legal systems have been the predominant sources for development of the administrative law of the European Community

[46] See W.P. Gormley, "The Significant Role of French Administrative Jurisprudence as Presently Applied by the Court of European Communities, With Emphasis on the Administrative Law Remedies Available to Private Litigants" (1963) 8 *South Dakota LR* 32; T. Koopmans, "The Birth of European Law at the Crossroads of Legal Traditions" (1991) 39 *American Journal of Comparative Law* 493; J. Schwarze, *European Administrative Law* (Sweet & Maxwell, London, 1992).

[47] See A. Bredimas, "Comparative Law in the Court of Justice of the European Communities", in *The Yearbook of World Affairs 1978 Volume 32* (Stevens, London, 1978), 320; P. Pescatore, "*Le Recourse, dans la Jurisprudence de la Cour de Justice des Communautés Européennes, a des Normes Déduites de la Comparison des Droits des États Membres*" (1980) 32 *Revue Internationale de Droit Comparé* 337; F. Jacobs, "The Uses of Comparative Law in the Law of the European Communities", in R. Plender (ed.), *Legal History and Comparative Law: Essays in Honour of Albert Kiralfy* (Frank Cass, London, 1990), 99.

[48] Case 14/61 *Koninklijke Nederlandsche Hoogovens en Staalfabrieken NV* v. *High Authority of the European Coal and Steel Community* [1962] ECR 253, 283–4 of Advocate-General Lagrange's opinion; Joined Cases 63 to 69/72 *Wilhelm Wehahn Hansamühle* v. *Council* [1973] ECR 1229, 1260 (col. 1) of Advocate-General Roemer's opinion. See also H. Kutscher, "Methods of Interpretation as Seen by a Judge at the Court of Justice", in *Judicial and Academic Conference 27–28 September 1976* (Luxembourg, 1976); Y. Galmot, "*Réflexions sur le recourse au droit comparé par la Cour de Justice des Communautés européenes*" (1990) 6 *Revue française droit administratif* 255.

compared with the limited influence of English law owing in part to the relatively late entry of the United Kingdom into the European Community. It is therefore necessary to examine the differences between these approaches to administrative law. In comparison with the English approach, administrative law on the Continent is characterised by a tradition of the state as a distinct legal entity, a division between public and private law, a purposive approach to judicial review and specialist administrative courts.[49]

The absence of an English state tradition contrasts sharply with the Continent. Both France and Germany have strong traditions of theorising over the role and purpose of the state and its relationship to law.[50] The significance of a state tradition is that it has provided an intellectual footing for administrative law. Just as England lacks any legal concept of the state, it also lacks a coherent system of administrative law. In Continental states administrative law is conceptualised differently; the administration is viewed as the institution which realises the purposes of the state, and a systematic and rational body of law is necessary to regulate the exercise of such power. Administration is conducted through a legal-rational method of bureaucracy, with legally trained administrators using formalised techniques of decision-making, whilst law provides values and principles to inform public action. Continental jurists recognised that the state possessed powers to perform unique tasks which resulted in an inequality between the individual and the state. Consequently, a distinct body of law was required to control and supervise state activities. The distinction between public law and private law, which had its roots in Roman law, became fundamental to the civil law tradition.[51] A substantive distinction was made between the principles regulating the state and relations between private individuals. For instance, in the *Blanco* case the French *Tribunal des Conflits* declared that the liability of the state was governed by a separate set of public law rules:[52]

> *"cette responsabilité n'est ni générale, ni absolue; qu'elle a ses règles spéciales qui varient suivant les besoins du service et la necessité de concilier les droit de l'État avec les droits privés".*

---

[49] On the European traditions of administrative law, see J. Bell, "Mechanisms for Cross-fertilisation of Administrative Law in Europe", in J. Beatson and T. Tridimas (eds), *New Directions in European Public Law* (Hart Publishing, Oxford, 1998), 147, 148–51.

[50] L. Duguit, "The Law and the State" (1917/18) 31 *Harvard LR* 1; N. Johnson, "Law as the Articulation of the State in Western Germany: A German tradition seen from a British Perspective" (1978) 1 *Western European Politics* 177; Dyson, above at n. 10, ch. 6; H.S. Jones, *The French State in Question: Public Law and Political Argument in the Third Republic* (Cambridge University Press, Cambridge, 1993), ch. 3.

[51] See C. Szladits, "The Civil Law System", in *International Encyclopedia of Comparative Law*, II–2 *Structure and the Divisions of the Law*, 15; A.E. Tay and E. Kamenka, "Public Law—Private Law", in S.I. Benn and G.F. Gaus (eds), *Public and Private in Social Life* (London, 1983), 67.

[52] *Tribunal des Conflits*, 8 February 1873, quoted from M. Long *et al.* (eds), *Les grands arrêts de la jurisprudence administrative* (Paris, Sirey, 10th ed. 1993), 1: "this liability is neither general nor absolute; that it has its own rules which vary according to the needs of the service and the necessity to reconcile the rights of the state with private rights".

A strict division between public and private law led to separate principles specifically designed for public law adjudication.

For Continental jurists the rule governing the whole of administrative law is the principle of the purpose pursued.[53] The administration acts in the public interest and the law must recognise its purposes. In the words of Maxime Letourneur, a former member of the *Conseil d'État*, "[a]dministrative law is, by its very nature, an unequal law; for the general interest must be accorded supremacy over private rights".[54] The role of the administrative judge is to reconcile the imperative requirements of the general interest with the legitimate interests of the individual by advising the administration upon its course of action. The underlying purpose of judicial control of the administration is to recognise the different needs of the state and the individual, and to balance them accordingly. The purpose of this balancing test is to ensure that in the exercise of its powers the state does not act arbitrarily towards individuals. According to Advocate-General Lagrange, it forms "one of the fundamental concepts of administrative law, and . . . [is] . . . without doubt the chief justification for the very existence of administrative courts".[55] In undertaking this balancing exercise the administrative court does not substitute its own assessment of discretionary choices for that of the administrator, but intervenes if a decision incurs abnormally high costs or is unreasonable or badly thought-out. This forces the administration to provide serious and plausible justifications for its decisions to the public and, if necessary, to the administrative judge.[56] According to the German jurist, Eberhard Schmidt-Aßmann, the most important feature of administrative law is its sensitivity: connections between state actions and private interests are investigated in respect of their intensity, extent and depth, and their rationality examined.[57]

The balancing test is a relative exercise dependent upon the competing strengths of the interests involved. There are no straightforward solutions on how the balance should be struck. In general, the public interest represented by respect for legality prevails; the only exception is where the administrative decision so interferes with private interests that the public interest cannot justify the incursion. When examining the balance struck the administrative court undertakes a judgment in light of the changing needs of public administration which is oriented towards the goal the administration wishes to achieve. One of the techniques used to enable the administrative court to balance the competing

---

[53] See, e.g., L. Duguit, *Law in the Modern State* (London, 1921), (translated by F. Laski and H.J. Laski), 142–4.

[54] M. Letourneur, "The Concept of Equity in French Public Law", in R.A. Newman (ed.), *Equity in the World's Legal Systems: A Comparative Study* (Brussels, 1973), 261, 262.

[55] Case 14/61 *Hoogovens*, above at n. 48, 283 (col. 1).

[56] See the opinion of Commissaire du Gouvernement Braibant in *Conseil d'État*, 28 May 1971, *Ville Nouvelle Est*, quoted in L. Neville Brown and J.S. Bell with the assistance of J.-M. Galabert, *French Administrative Law* (Clarendon Press, Oxford, 5th ed. 1998), 264.

[57] E. Schmidt-Aßmann, "Basic Principles of German Administrative Law" (1993) 35 *Journal of the Indian Law Institute* 65, 69.

interests has been to develop general principles of law to enforce an administrative morality. The state is required to act honestly and behave properly towards its citizens.[58] Such principles are specifically designed to resolve disputes between individuals and the state in light of the conflict between public objective and individual interests.

In Continental states, specialist administrative courts were established to apply administrative laws to developing state structures. In France, the *Conseil d'État* gradually evolved as an independent jurisdiction for administrative adjudication operating through inquisitorial procedures.[59] In Germany an independent system of administrative courts[60] has developed to uphold the *Rechtsstaat* concept, i.e. the notion that a constitutional state can exist only through the rule of law.[61] It is, of course, extremely difficult to generalise about such institutions. The *Conseil d'État* occupies a unique position within the structure of French administration which is largely a product of its own history and could not easily be replicated elsewhere. Equally, administrative courts were established in Germany as a response to a specific crisis of legitimacy within that state, a fact reflected in the intensive scrutiny of administrative discretion exercised by its courts.[62] However, a common theme of these separate jurisdictions has been to allow a degree of specialisation in governmental processes that is simply unattainable in the ordinary courts. The Continental distinction between public and private law is closely connected to the existence of separate jurisdictions. With the growth in state activity at the beginning of the twentieth century, the French jurist, Léon Duguit, described this new approach to administrative law:[63]

> "The administration of the state is conducted under the control of administrative courts . . . Cognisant of the conditions under which it is necessary to operate the state they afford the necessary guarantees of independence and impartiality. They reconcile the interests of the state with those of private citizens. In this way all administration is a matter of law and controlled by the courts."

While the above similarities can be drawn, there are significant differences between French and German administrative law. The French tradition is based

---

[58] See Brown and Bell, above at n. 56, 214.

[59] See Hamson, above at n. 33; Brown and Bell, above at n. 56; J. Bell, "Reflections on the Procedure of the Conseil d'État", in G. Hand and J. McBride (eds), *Droit Sans Frontiers: Essays in Honour of L Neville Brown* (Holdsworth Club, Birmingham, 1991), 211.

[60] M.P. Singh, *German Administrative Law in Common Law Perspective* (Springer-Verlag, Berlin, 1985), ch. 7; B. Goller and A. Schmidt, "Reform of the German Administrative Courts Act" (1998) 4 *EPL* 31.

[61] See R.C. van Caenegem, "The 'Rechtsstaat' in Historical Perspective", in *Legal History: A European Perspective* (The Hambledon Press, London, 1991), 165; V. Götz, "Legislative and Executive Power under the Constitutional Requirements Entailed in the Principle of the Rule of Law", in C. Starck (ed.), *New Challenges to the German Basic Law* (Nomos Verlagsgesellschaft, Baden-Baden, 1991), 141.

[62] See E.K. Pakuscher, "The Use of Discretion in German Law" (1976–77) 44 *University of Chicago LR* 94; G. Nolte, "General Principles of German and European Administrative Law—A Comparison in Historical Perspective" (1994) 57 *MLR* 191.

[63] Duguit, above at n. 53, 158–9.

on the objective control of the legality of administrative action, and has been viewed as too oriented in favour of the administration.[64] Since the administration serves the public interest, French jurists have considered that it should not be constrained by a rigid set of rules, but by such limitations necessary to protect the individual in light of the needs of public administration. The distinctiveness of the *Conseil d'État* arises from the fact that it forms part of the administration itself and acts as both an adviser to government and an adjudicator in disputes brought by individuals.[65] As notions of legality are developed in response to the needs of the administration, the division between administration and adjudication, so important in the common law, does not have the same relevance in French law.

The German tradition is marked by a high degree of legalism in politics. Judicial review is dominated by the idea of the protection of the subjective rights of individuals and the control of discretionary power.[66] The intensity of review operated by German courts, particularly in the latter half of the twentieth century, is a consequence of the desire to control the state and protect individual rights. For German jurists administrative law is a "notion of order which has a lasting impact on the administrative culture".[67] In light of the constitutional declaration that the Federal Republic of Germany is a social state, as opposed to a liberal or individualistic state, administrative law has become one tool of contributing towards the effective administration of social welfare. German administrative law therefore aims at achieving an optimum balance between administrative effectiveness and the realisation of social interests, on the one hand, and the safeguard of individual interests, on the other. In order that administrative courts can effectively engage in the double mission of protection of the individual and efficiency of the administration in equal measure, a distinctive, purposive orientation is seen as necessary. In the opinion of Schmidt-Aßmann, "[a]n administrative law which does not recognise . . . [the] . . . legitimate functions of the administration . . . can . . . [only marginally] . . . influence . . . administrative reality".[68] Under the *Rechtsstaat* principle, German courts have developed the principles of legitimate expectations (*vertrauensschutz*) and proportionality (*verhältnismäßigkeit*) to regulate the citizen-state relationship. According to Günter Frankenberg, the purpose of administrative law is to juridify the sphere of state action by transforming relationships of power between the individual and the state into relationships of law.[69] Judicial

---

[64] See A. Mestre, *Le Conseil d'État: Proteurs des Privileges de l'Administration* (Librairie générale du droit française, 1974).

[65] See N. Questiaux, "Administration and the Rule of Law: The Preventative Role of the French Conseil d'État" [1995] *PL* 247.

[66] See A. Blankenagel, "The Concept of Subjective Rights as the Focal Point of German Administrative Law" (1992) 11 *Tel Aviv University Studies in Law* 79; P. Rädler, "Judicial Protection Against the Executive by German Administrative Courts" [1992] *Admin. Review* 78.

[67] E. Schmidt-Aßmann, quoted in Singh, above at n. 60, 2.

[68] Schmidt-Aßmann, above at n. 57, 66.

[69] G. Frankenberg, "Remarks on the Philosophy and Politics of Public Law" (1998) 18 *LS* 177, 179.

control is therefore correlative with the extent of administrative power. Furthermore, administrative law also provides specific rules which "concretise the overall purposive rationality of state action and rationalise state interventions into the social sphere".[70] Law legitimises the exercise of public power by subjecting it to control, but it also ensures the purposive efficacy of public decisions and rationalises their impact on individuals. In particular, the principle of proportionality is used to ensure sensitivity in public administration. For German jurists, therefore, the degree of legalism in politics is, in part, a function of the importance of social purposes and the need to ensure acceptability of administrative decisions by protecting values such as clarity, certainty and trustworthiness: "only a legally controlled and structured administration will be in the position of performing its functions in the long run".[71] In common with French law the division between law and administration is not as rigid as it is in English law; administration is not to be separated from law but can be properly conducted only if it subject to legal processes which recognise its distinctive nature.

COMPARING LEGAL TRADITIONS

The divergence between English and Continental traditions of public law has long been a theme of comparative scholarship. In 1903 it was noted that Continental public law "forms so complete an antithesis to the development of the law and constitution of England [that] the true meaning and effect . . . [of the latter] . . . are best shown" through this antithesis.[72] Writing in 1969, Mitchell was of the opinion that "[t]he critical gap between British and Continental laws . . . [was] . . . not in private, but in public law".[73] Certainly, profound differences in administrative law exist between England and the Continent. The different orientation towards law and administration stems, in part, from different administrative cultures in England and the Continent. The legalistic attitude of the Continental legal-rational model of bureaucracy is almost the polar opposite of the traditionally more pragmatic, discretion-based approach of the British administrator. This difference in administrative culture infuses methods of redress against government. In Continental states, lawyers have an established role in administration, and law is seen as a necessary feature of the administrative process, whereas British lawyers have tended to occupy a marginal role in government. The Continental approach places importance on legal remedies for individuals, whereas in Britain the primary focus is redress through political channels with courts playing a subsidiary role. In the early

---

[70] Ibid., 180.

[71] Schmidt-Aßmann, above at n. 57, 77.

[72] Redlich and Hirst, above at n. 11, 325.

[73] J.D.B. Mitchell, "Why European Institutions?", in L.J. Brinkhorst and J.D.B. Mitchell, *European Law and Institutions* (Edinburgh University Press, Edinburgh, 1969), 30, 36.

1970s, Sir Leslie Scarman commented that the sovereignty of Parliament has meant that, in practice, ministers and their advisers have viewed Parliament as the only place to explain and defend policies and their implementation: "[t]heir attention to the law has never really gone further than the regard necessary to keep the department out of the courts".[74] Since then, judges have felt compelled to strengthen judicial controls because the accountability of government by Parliament has "on occasion been perceived as falling short, and sometimes well short, of what was needed to bring the performance of the executive into line with the law, and with the minimum standards of fairness".[75] The growth in judicial review has therefore been prompted by a desire "[t]o avoid a vacuum in which the citizen would be left without protection against a misuse of executive powers",[76] as opposed to the purposeful rationalisation of state activity through law.

The rational and systematic approach of Continental legal orders to the protection of the individual and administrative efficiency contrasts sharply with the anti-rationalist common law method. Continental states view law as a means of administration specifically designed to enable the administration to perform its functions. For Otto Kahn-Freund this difference was rooted in political history and reflected in the fact that in Continental states, government has an inherent power to govern, whereas in the common law government lacks any inherent power:[77]

> "That which is true of administrative action under the common law—that it must be based on a statutory grant of power—is true of judicial action under the 'civil law' systems."

The inherent power of common law courts has allowed them to develop their power of review from their traditional authority of supervising the decisions of inferior bodies. The common law style of reasoning from precedent and using the artificial reason of law is bound up intimately with the inherent jurisdiction of courts. In comparison, the power of Continental administrative courts is dependent upon legislation which regulates their jurisdiction. Accordingly, they operate within a more formal and rational framework to contribute towards the achievement of social purposes through law. The basic definition given to administrative law is also reflected in institutions, such as administrative courts. On the Continent, specialist administrative jurisdictions are seen as necessary to the process of the juridification of power relationships in light of the increasing complexity and scale of the modern state. By comparison, issues of public law in England were resolved by ordinary courts applying ordinary common law

---

[74] Sir Leslie Scarman, "Law and Administration: A Change in Relationship" (1972) 50 *Public Administration* 253, 256.

[75] *R. v. Secretary of State for the Home Department, ex parte Fire Brigades Union* [1995] 2 WLR 464, 488B–C, *per* Lord Mustill (dissenting).

[76] Ibid., 488C.

[77] O. Kahn-Freund, "Common Law and Civil Law—Imaginary and Real Obstacles to Assimilation", in M. Cappelletti (ed.), *New Perspectives For a Common Law of Europe* (Sijthoff, Leyden, 1978), 137, 160.

rules. As a close relationship exists between Continental administrators and courts there is a better fusion of fairness, with good and efficient administration, than in common law where, in the absence of such a relationship, the courts concentrate only on imposing standards of fairness on the administration. In Continental states administrative law developed as an autonomous and systematic discipline, with separate legal principles regulating the relationship between citizens and the state. In England, on the other hand, the common law has traditionally emphasised the universality of the law.

Significantly different styles of legal reasoning and approach exist between the pragmatic common law tradition and the more formal and rational civilian tradition. J.S. Mill's comment that the English "distrust everything which emanates from general principles . . . [while] . . . the French . . . distrust whatever does not so emanate" is indicative of the different habits of legal thought.[78] Continental legal systems have endeavoured to keep step with evolving governmental activities and maintain a rational public law by relating judgments to principles derived from an evolving philosophy of the state. In England, the growth of government has exceeded the limits of the law, and common law became caught up in a web of governmental immunities and concepts which have prevented the evolution of a coherent body of law.

The relationship between English and Continental approaches to administrative law has developed over time. English law has been able to define itself by reference to Continental systems, in particular *droit administratif*. When Dicey first made the comparison he could comfortably assert the superiority of common law values. The dignified and majestic culture of the common law was viewed as a better protector of the individual because it did not allow the government any special legal treatment. It was precisely this distaste for viewing law as a necessary feature of state activity that led Lord Hewart to opine that the "Continental system of 'Administrative Law' . . . [was] . . . profoundly repugnant . . . to English ideas".[79] However, as the growth in administrative power continued, comparative studies undermined the view that English law provided better protection for the individual.[80] As Mario Chiti has explained, the development of a separate administrative law in Continental states did not imply that the administration was exempt from control:[81]

"rather . . . it was subject to an administrative legality which was distinct in content and conditions from the law to which private individuals were subject. This was

---

[78] J.S. Mill, "Bentham" (1838), in J.S. Mill and J. Bentham, *Utilitarianism and Other Essays* (Penguin, Harmondsworth, 1987), 132, 164.

[79] Lord Hewart, above at n. 31, 12–13.

[80] See F.J. Port, *Administrative Law* (London, 1929), ch. VII; B. Schwartz, *French Administrative Law and the Common-Law World* (University Press, New York, 1954), ch. 10; Hamson, above at n. 33; J.W.F. Allison, *A Continental Distinction in the Common Law: A Historical and Comparative Perspective on English Public Law* (Clarendon Press, Oxford, 1996), ch. 8.

[81] M.P. Chiti, "Administrative Comparative Law" (1992) 4 *European Review of Public Law* 11, 19.

perhaps a more efficient means of limiting administrative power, for it was modelled on the specific characteristics of that power, in a continuous dialectic between authority and liberty."

The response of Continental systems to state activity has been positive: notions of legality have been adapted to the changing purposes of the administration. The development of Continental administrative law has been characterised by the change of focus "from administrative power to administrative function" with the law based not just on the idea of control but also on the values of efficiency and impartiality.[82] In comparison, English law has failed to provide an adequate response to such pressures, preferring to retain the traditional common law approach. The extent that English judges have responded to the Continental belief that England lacks an administrative law has been by recourse to the upsurge in applications for judicial review and the establishment of a separate procedure. However, the common law conception of legality continues to hold a compelling embrace on the judicial mind-set.[83] This is in sharp contrast with the French, who:[84]

"find a justification for the distinct character of their *droit administratif* in its capacity to adapt the principles of administrative legality and administrative liability to the differing needs of the various public services, a capacity which they claim could only be found in judges who are also trained administrators."

The common law conception of legality is also in contrast with German administrative law which lays stress on the importance of substantive controls over discretionary power by specialist courts to rationalise the effects of public decisions on individuals.

EUROPEAN COMMUNITY ADMINISTRATIVE LAW

European Community administrative law is a unique hybrid of different legal traditions specifically adapted for the purposes of the Community.[85] The European Court of Justice has adopted the principles of legitimate expectations and proportionality into its review of administrative legality. In order to appreciate the different roles of law in the Community and in Britain it is necessary to interpret what is implied within the basic conception of law. To do this it is

---

[82] G. Arena, "Rights vis-à-vis the Administration: Commentary", in A. Cassese, A. Clapham and J. Weiler (eds), *Human Rights and the European Community: Methods of Protection* (Nomos Verlagsgesellschaft, Baden-Baden, 1991), 495, 498–502.

[83] See G. Slynn, "But in England there is no . . ." in W. Fuerst (ed.), *Festschrift für Wolfgang Zeidler Volume 1* (Berlin/New York, 1987), 397; Lord Woolf of Barnes, "Droit Public—English Style" [1995] PL 57.

[84] Brown and Bell, above at n. 56, 291–2.

[85] See C. Harlow, "European Administrative Law and the Global Challenge", in P.P. Craig and G. de Búrca, *The Evolution of EU Law* (Clarendon Press, Oxford, 1999), 261.

useful to consider the work of Michael Oakeshott concerning the ideal nature of the civil condition.[86]

Oakeshott considers that there are two categorically discrete modes of human relationship: enterprise association and civil association. Enterprise association exists for the pursuit of a common purpose or interest. The relationships in the association are defined by the identification of the common purpose and the managerial decisions which are taken to further this purpose. The rules of the association are contingently related to the purpose concerned and are designed to promote its realisation. The second mode of human relationship, civil association, is distinct from the first because its members are not concerned with the pursuit of any common purpose of interest but are related in terms of a practice. Civil association is a formal and rule-based association in which members can pursue their own individual interests within the framework of its rules. These rules constitute the practice of civility of the association and are therefore non-purposive. Whereas the rules of an enterprise association are determined by their instrumental functionality, in a civil association the rules are unrelated to any common purpose, because there is none. Members acknowledge each other through the recognition of a practice composed of rules which prescribe their common responsibilities and formal equality.

According to Oakeshott, the civil condition is to be understood as an association in terms of a practice. In other words, the state is a form of civil association and its law is non-purposive, existing through the continuous recognition of the authority of common practices. As regards the British state, the traditional conception of public law would appear to endorse this characterisation of the state as a form of civil association, which most clearly explains British traditions. For instance, Acts of Parliament do not identify the purposes for which they were adopted, and courts adjudicate through analogical reasoning acting as the custodians of the law. By contrast, the European Community would appear to be more appropriately classified as an enterprise association. The European Treaties have entrenched the values of economic liberalism at a constitutional level, and the European Court acts as the guardian of the Treaties by promoting the integrationist purposes of the Community.[87] Community administration is conducted through purpose-driven regulations and rules adopted for identified objectives. This contrasts with the greater reliance on wide discretionary powers exercised by British administrators.

The importance of the basic conception of the nature of the polity is that it leads to different conceptions of law. In a civil association, law courts are concerned with the meaning of law in a contingent situation. As there is no common purpose to the association the meaning of law is not deduced but is always

---

[86] M. Oakeshott, *On Human Conduct* (Clarendon Press, Oxford, 1975), Part II, "On the Civil Condition". See also M. Oakeshott, "The Rule of Law", in *On History and other essays* (Blackwell, Oxford, 1983), 119.

[87] G.F. Mancini and D.T. Keeling, "Democracy and the European Court of Justice" (1994) 57 *MLR* 175, 186. See also R. Dehousse, *The European Court of Justice* (Macmillan, London, 1998).

attributed or given. For example, the review exercised by English courts for unreasonableness does not seek to promote the purposes of governance; such purposes are not usually identified. Rather, the courts engage in an exercise in retrospective casuistry by asking whether a decision was so unreasonable that no reasonable authority could every have arrived at it.[88]

By contrast, in an enterprise association the resolution of disputes is achieved by agreement on managerial decisions concerning the pursuit of the purposes of the association. The adjudication of disputes is conceived of as a means of realising and implementing social policy. For example, if a political authority decides to intervene in the social sphere in order to realise a certain end, then review of the proportionality of that decision examines whether the intervention was suitable and necessary in light of the policy objective to be achieved. Adjudication is a form of managerial decision concerning the common goals of the association.

The relevance of this discussion is that it demonstrates how our basic understanding of the civil condition as either an enterprise association or a civil association influences how we think about law. The European Community is a pre-eminent example of an enterprise association, and its law is closely connected with the achievement of its purpose; whereas the British state is usually conceived of as a civil association in which law is separate from governmental purposes. While Oakeshott's distinction is an idealisation, it is submitted that it demonstrates the essential difference between the European Community and the British state, and the different roles of law.

The jurisprudence of the European Court reflects these ideas. While the methodology and style of the European Court is the result of different legal traditions, it has developed grounds of review by adopting a purposive orientation towards the exercise of public power. Early in the court's jurisprudence, Advocate-General Lagrange signalled that the orientation of Community administrative law would be guided by the purposes of the Community:[89]

> "[T]he rule which governs the whole of administrative law . . . [is] . . . the principle of the purpose pursued. In contrast to the rights of private individuals . . . the rights of public authorities which are in fact powers, may be exercised only for the *purposes* for which they have been vested with those powers . . . [T]hese purposes are . . . the public interest, what is called the 'good of the service' for which the Administration was created and which is nothing other than the embodiment of the social good which is the foundation of social order."

While the European Court was at first disinclined to exercise a thorough review of legality of decisions adopted by the institutions, it has developed general principles of law to guide and control the Community administration in its dealings

---

[88] *Associated Provincial Picture Houses Ltd.* v. *Wednesbury Corporation* [1948] 1 KB 223.
[89] Case 3/54 *Associazone Industrie Siderurgiche Italiane (ASSIDER)* v. *High Authority of the European Coal and Steel Community* [1954–56] ECR 63, 76 (col. 1) of the Advocate-General's opinion.

with individuals and traders.[90] Conscious that the general principles of law will need to be applied across a diverse range of administrative powers that change with the development of the Community, the European Court has left room for further interpretation, precision and elaboration of the principles. For some commentators the importance of the general principles is such that they should be codified.[91]

European Community administrative law is an amalgam of different influences and visions of what constitutes "administrative law". While the Continental approach has provided the intellectual background for the development of Community administrative law, the common law has also provided some, albeit limited, influence.[92] It would be a mistake to assume a high degree of homogeneity between Community administrative law and Continental conceptions. In the opinion of Louis Dubouis, Community administrative law has proceeded on the basis of a narrower conception of administrative law than is normally adopted in France and Germany.[93] For instance, from a German perspective the European Court adopts a less-intensive form of substantive review than the searching scrutiny undertaken by German administrative courts to avoid any undue interference with the decision-making competence of Community institutions.[94] At the same time, there is a special connection between the administrative law of the European Community and those of some Continental states. According to Georg Nolte, a distinctive relationship between German and European administrative law has arisen because of the striking similarity in the use of the principles, such as legitimate expectations and proportionality, even though the European Court prefers not to subject public decisions to such a searching review as the German courts.[95]

[90] See W. Lorenz, "General Principles of Law: Their Elaboration in the Court of Justice of the European Communities" (1964) 13 *American Journal of Comparative Law* 1; M. Akehurst, "The Application of General Principles of Law by the Court of Justice of the European Communities" (1981) 52 *BYIL* 29; J.A. Usher, *General Principles of EC Law* (Longman, London, 1998).

[91] See J. Schwarze, "The Europeanization of National Administrative Law", in J. Schwarze (ed.), *Administrative Law Under European Influence: On the convergence of the administrative laws of the EU Member States* (Sweet & Maxwell, London, 1996), 789, 830–6.

[92] See Case 17/74 *Transocean Marine Paint Association* v. *Commission* [1974] ECR 1063 (the right to be heard); Case 155/79 *AM & S Europe* v. *Commission* [1982] ECR 1575 (legal professional privilege). See also J. Bell, "The English Lawyer in the Europe of 1993" (1991/2) 34 *University of Leeds Review* 181.

[93] L. Dubouis, "*Le droit communautaire a-t-il un impact sur la définition du droit administratif?*" [1996] *Actualité Juridique: Droit Administratif* 102, 108 (special edition entitled *Droit Administratif et Droit Communautaire. Des influences réciproques à la perspective d'un droit administratif européen: les données du débat contemporain*).

[94] T. Jakob, "The rule of law", in C.-C. Schweitzer and D. Karsten (eds), *The Federal Republic of Germany and EC Membership Evaluated* (Pinter, London, 1990), 161, 164; M. Brenner, "Administrative Judicial Protection in Europe: General Principles" (1997) 9 *European Review of Public Law* 595, 615.

[95] Nolte, above at n. 61, 211.

CONCLUSION

This chapter has examined the approaches to the role of law in public administration in England and Continental Europe. It will be evident that the intention
has been to identify the general orientations that underlie English and European
administrative law rather than give a detailed account of their specifics. It has
been seen that these approaches have developed within different historical and
legal traditions. Clearly, it is important not to exaggerate the differences
between English and Continental approaches to administrative law. Systems of
administrative law are intimately connected with national styles of administration and, as such, there will always be differences of approach and emphasis.
However, whereas Continental states have sought to respond constructively to
the "juridification of the social world",[96] English law has preferred to retain an
informal common law conception of legality. This divergence of approach to
basic social changes in the state has influenced the different orientation towards
the role of law in administration between England and the Continent.
Transcending the differences between *droit administratif* and *verwaltungsrecht*
is the recognition that law should play a socially beneficial role in public administration by the purposeful rationalisation of public decisions. This underlying
orientation is also reflected in the development of the administrative law of the
European Community.

What this chapter demonstrates is that there are significantly different starting points for the debate over the principles of legitimate expectations and proportionality between England and the European Community owing to the
underlying approaches to administrative law. It is to these styles of thought that
reference will be made when comparing the development of the principles in the
jurisprudence of the English courts and the European Court of Justice.

---

[96] See, generally, G. Teubner (ed.), *Dilemmas of Law in the Welfare State* (de Gruyter,
Berlin/New York, 1985).

2

The Integration of the Principles into English Law

WHY HAVE THE ENGLISH courts increasingly referred to the principles of legitimate expectations and proportionality over the last few decades? What has been the impetus behind these important legal developments? This chapter will explain why English judges have introduced these two principles into their justificatory language. It is contended here that there have been two different forms of pressure for the development of the principles in English law. An internal pressure has been exerted by members of the judiciary themselves who have been proactive in introducing these new principles into English law. This form of influence can be seen most clearly in the role of Lord Diplock. At the same time, an external impetus for change in the form of the increasing importance of European Community law has brought the principles to the judges' attention.

In 1963 Lord Reid remarked that "[w]e do not have a developed system of administrative law—perhaps because until fairly recently we did not need it".[1] With the growth in the scale and complexity of state activity in the post-war period the judiciary were increasingly being called upon to resolve novel problems concerning the exercise of public power. However, the courts were unprepared for the new types of cases coming before them. As Lord Reid continued, in dealing with these new cases, "the courts have had to grope for solutions, and have found that old powers, rules and procedures are largely inapplicable to cases which they were never designed or intended to deal with".[2] This statement precisely captures the quandary facing the English courts, namely, how to develop distinct principles of public law out of the common law, a legal culture which has traditionally emphasised the generality of the law and rejected the idea that governance requires special legal consideration.

Is it possible that English judges were tempted to look elsewhere for guidance? At first glance, the answer to this would appear to be "no"; after all, the common law is the product of the accumulated experience of judges, and principles

[1] *Ridge v. Baldwin* [1964] AC 40, 72.
[2] Ibid., 73.

that do not derive from such knowledge are unlikely to appeal to English judges. For instance, it was Lord Denning who first referred to "legitimate expectation" in 1969, and who also employed the notion of proportionality.[3] However, Lord Denning noted subsequently that the reference to legitimate expectation came from his own mind and not from any other source.[4] He also considered that Continental-style systems of administrative law allowed the executive to shelter from the full rigour of the law.[5] However, the principles of legitimate expectation and proportionality were manifestly not inventions of the common law. Having originated in German public law, they came to be accepted by the European Court of Justice as "progressive" public law concepts.[6] How, then, did they come to gain acceptance in English law? To find an answer to this it is necessary to examine the attitude of English judiciary generally, and of Lord Diplock in particular.

The development of judicial review of administrative action in Britain is well-documented. Following the lead taken by the House of Lords in a number of important cases,[7] other judges have been encouraged to develop the common law. The courts have undertaken a major project in which old remedies have been resurrected and obstacles removed in order to provide individuals with a means of redress to ensure that government acts lawfully. Reform of the procedures of judicial review in the late 1970s prompted the need for clearer articulation of the principles used by judges in examining public decision-making. As Sir Henry Maine once noted, the principles of law are "gradually secreted in the interstices of procedure".[8] The general shift in the practice of judicial review has reflected a move from a deferential to a more intensive review of public decision-making by judges, which prompted the need for coherent principles. If judges were to play a greater role in reviewing the decisions of public authorities, they needed to be able to justify their reasoning by reference to general principles. These forces created a general trend towards the formalisation of legal principle. But what was the specific impetus behind the development of legitimate expectations and proportionality in English law?

While most judges worked within established precedent, one judge, Lord Diplock, consciously attempted to develop new solutions to enable the courts to resolve disputes brought before them. Lord Diplock was a Law Lord from 1968 to 1985 and exerted a powerful influence over the development of administra-

---

[3] *Schmidt* v. *Secretary of State for Home Affairs* [1969] 2 Ch 149; *R.* v. *Barnsley Metropolitan Borough Council, ex parte Hook* [1976] 1 WLR 1052.

[4] Lord Denning, quoted in C.F. Forsyth, "The Provenance and Protection of Legitimate Expectations" (1988) 47 *CLJ* 238, 241.

[5] *Ministry of Housing and Local Government* v. *Sharp* [1970] 2 QB 223, 266D.

[6] Cf. Case 14/61 *Koninklijke Nederlandsche Hoogovens en Staalfabrieken NV* v. *High Authority of the European Coal and Steel Community* [1962] ECR 253, 284 (col. 1) of the opinion of Advocate-General Lagrange.

[7] *Ridge* v. *Baldwin*, above at n. 1; *Padfield* v. *Minister of Agriculture, Fisheries and Food* [1968] AC 997; *Anisminic Ltd.* v. *Foreign Compensation Commission* [1969] 2 AC 147.

[8] Sir Henry Maine, *Dissertations on Early Law and Custom* (John Murray, London, 1883), 389.

tive law.[9] As Sir Stephen Sedley has noted, Lord Diplock "never uttered a word without some carefully thought-out purpose".[10] What role did Lord Diplock play in the integration of the two principles into English law?

In 1977 Lord Diplock ended his address to the Fifth Commonwealth Law Conference with a review of the development of judicial review. For Lord Diplock this had been "the great achievement of the twentieth century in the judicial development of the law".[11] Recalling his admiration of the nineteenth century judges who had succeeded in adapting private law to the needs of industrial society, Lord Diplock opined that the gradual development of judicial review had been equally successful in adapting law to the needs of contemporary society. Lord Diplock concluded by stating that public law now rivalled private law in the influence it has on human happiness and well-being: "[a]nd, if I have my way, we have not finished yet".[12] Earlier the same year Lord Diplock indicated the course of direction he had in mind for English law. In a contribution to a House of Lords debate on the introduction of a Bill of Rights, he referred to the European context of the forms of protection for fundamental rights.[13] Recalling a meeting of the heads of the supreme administrative courts of the Member States of the European Community at The Hague, Lord Diplock reported that it had been the unanimous opinion of all that the grounds of a breach of fundamental rights would have substantially the same result in all European countries.[14] In referring to Community law Lord Diplock recognised that although the European Treaty did not contain any explicit guarantee concerning fundamental rights, the European Court had not taken the lowest common measure but had looked to the more progressive doctrines in the national

---

[9] On Diplock's judicial career, see R. Stevens, *Law and Politics: the House of Lords as a Judicial Body, 1800–1976* (Weidenfeld and Nicolson, London, 1979), 565–9; B. Dickson, "The Contribution of Lord Diplock to the General Law of Contract" (1989) 9 *OJLS* 441, 442–4. Lord Diplock was a powerful judge whose judgments were characterised by their penetrating analyses and precise use of language. However, his intellectual confidence could, on occasion, lead to ironic put-downs. For example, in *Hughes* v. *Hughes* (1966) unreported, sitting in the Court of Appeal with Lord Denning MR and Harman LJ, who both favoured the appeal, Lord (then Lord Justice) Diplock dissented simply by stating: "[f]or the reasons given by my brother Harman, I would dismiss the appeal": L. Blom-Cooper and G. Drewry, *Final Appeal: A Study of the House of Lords in its Judicial Capacity* (Clarendon Press, Oxford, 1972), 87.

[10] S. Sedley, "The Sound of Silence: Constitutional Law Without a Constitution" (1994) 110 *LQR* 270, 282. Elsewhere, Sir Stephen Sedley has described Lord Diplock as "the judge who perhaps more than any other deserves recognition as the engineer, if not quite the architect, of modern public law . . . and to whom the throwaway remark was a foreign concept": "The Common Law and the Constitution", *London Review of Books*, 8 May 1997, 8, 9.

[11] Lord Diplock, "Judicial Development of Law in the Commonwealth", in *Proceedings and Papers of the Fifth Commonwealth Law Conference* (Blackwood, Edinburgh, 1978), 493, 500.

[12] Ibid.

[13] *Hansard*, H.L. Deb., Vol. 379, cols 991–5, 3 February 1977.

[14] Fifth Colloquium of the Councils of State and the Supreme Courts of Justice of the Member States of the European Communities, *Discretionary Power and the Advisability of Administrative Decisions; The Extent and Limitations of Judicial Control* (Government Publishing Control, The Hague, 1976). Commenting on his own attendance, Lord Diplock remarked that "[m]ay be I went under a false trade description bearing in mind Dicey's proud disclaimer that *droit administratif* formed any part of English or Imperial law": Lord Diplock, above at n. 11, 500.

legal systems. As a result of this method the European Court had developed two doctrines "which have not yet been accepted fully in this country".[15] The two doctrines were legitimate expectations and proportionality. In a revealing aside, Lord Diplock intimated that "[t]hose are the two that I had in mind particularly as doctrines which are only just beginning to be assimilated in this country".[16] In other words, Lord Diplock considered the time had arrived for judicial development of the two principles in English law.

It is important to understand the motivation behind this project. However, in attempting to do so an immediate difficulty emerges; Lord Diplock did not provide any clear explanation of why he considered the assimilation of the principles into English law. In an attempt to bring to light an underlying coherence this section will advance possible interpretations of Lord Diplock's conduct. By piecing together what little information exists, Lord Diplock's intention to develop these principles in English law can be subjected to a range of different interpretations in order to find a coherence between his actions and the meaning of the situation for him.

The first interpretation is that the adoption of the principles of legitimate expectations and proportionality was viewed as a further movement towards a developed administrative law. The "breakthrough"[17] of *Anisminic* had freed the courts from drawing technical distinctions between errors of law within and without jurisdiction. In *Ridge* v. *Baldwin* the House of Lords revived and expanded the applicability of the right to be heard. Following the procedural reforms of RSC Order 53, Lord Diplock introduced a principle of procedural exclusivity as regards applications for judicial review and used the terms "public law" and "private law" to signify the difference between the proceedings.[18] Referring to the statement of Lord Reid concerning the lack of an English system of administrative law, Lord Diplock commented that:[19]

"[b]y 1977 the need . . . [for an administrative law] . . . had continued to grow apace and this reproach to English law had been removed. We did have by then a developed system of administrative law".

The assimilation of the new principles could have been viewed as a fulfilment of Lord Reid's challenge for the courts to find new solutions to the new cases coming before them.[20] Central to the developing system of administrative law was the elaboration of grounds of review, and the new principles could therefore be viewed as part of the rationalisation and simplification of judicial review desired by Lord Diplock.

---

[15] *Hansard*, above at n. 12, col. 993.

[16] Ibid., col. 994.

[17] *In re Racal Communications Ltd.* [1981] AC 374, 383B, *per* Lord Diplock.

[18] Supreme Court Act 1981, s. 31; *O'Reilly* v. *Mackman* [1983] 2 AC 237.

[19] Ibid., 283H–285G. See also Lord Diplock, "Judicial Control of Administrative Action" (1971) 24 *CLP* 1; Lord Diplock, "Administrative Law: Judicial Review Reviewed" (1974) 22 *CLJ* 233.

[20] J.A.G. Griffith, *Judicial Politics Since 1920: A Chronicle* (Blackwell, Oxford, 1993), 148, describes Lord Diplock, alongside Lord Wilberforce, as "positivists in their approach to law carrying forward the Reid tradition".

Lord Diplock could also have been motivated by a general desire for English law to keep up with Continental developments. He was certainly interested in comparative law and well aware of the case law of the *Conseil d'État* and the German Federal Administrative Court (*Bundesverwaltungsgericht*), as well as the European Court.[21] Even before the United Kingdom joined the European Community Lord Diplock had remarked that:[22]

> "[i]n the course of my lifetime in the law, I have been fortunate to work enough with European lawyers to believe that the common law has much to gain from closer contact with and understanding of the concepts of the civil law."

In the opinion of Lord Wilberforce there were two features in Lord Diplock's approach: first, cautious moves within established principle and secondly, a desire to keep English law in a moving relationship with European developments.[23] According to Sir William Wade, Lord Diplock's "object was to show that British judicial review was fully equal to that of other countries in range and effectiveness".[24]

Significantly, the meeting at The Hague of the supreme administrative courts of Europe focused upon the judicial control of discretionary power. In his welcoming address, W.F. De Gaay Fortman set the tone of the conference by remarking that:[25]

> "[t]he growing integration of the European Communities means that the . . . [national courts] . . . must pay ever closer attention to the administrative law of the other Member States and also to the jurisprudence evolved by the Court of Justice . . . Mutual influences are at work here."

The introduction of legitimate expectations and proportionality was not preceded by any direct exposure of English law to the Community principles. However, it is clear that Lord Diplock's interest in European and comparative law provided an impetus for developing similar principles in English law. Furthermore, it seems likely that Lord Diplock appreciated the importance of the European Community and its potential influence on English law. By his own

---

[21] See, e.g., Lord Diplock, "Preface", in J.F. Garner and A.R. Galbraith (eds), *Judicial Control of the Administrative Process* (Report of a Conference at Ditchley Park, 4–7 July 1969, Ditchley Paper No. 22); Lord Diplock, "Foreword", in B. Schwartz and H.W.R. Wade, *Legal Control of Government* (Clarendon Press, Oxford, 1972), xi. Lord Diplock acted a chairman in the Seventh Colloquium of the Councils of State and the Supreme Courts of Justice of Member States of the European Community, *The Power of the Courts—both Superior and Inferior Courts and Bodies Exercising Quasi-Judicial Functions—to Award Damages in Administrative Actions* (London, 1980). In his opening address he stated, at 193: "[t]he topic that we have chosen . . . (and I must confess I have a certain share of the responsibility for choosing it) is a branch of administrative law where I think that we in the United Kingdom perhaps have the greatest amount to learn from you".

[22] Lord Diplock, "The Common Market and the Common Law" (1972) 6 *The Law Teacher* 3, 16.

[23] Lord Wilberforce, "Lord Diplock and Administrative Law" [1986] *PL* 6.

[24] Letter from Sir William Wade to the author dated 26 March 1997.

[25] *Discretionary Power and the Advisability of Administrative Decisions; The Extent and Limitations of Judicial Control*, above at n. 14, 197.

admission, Lord Diplock was "interested in the legal questions involved in membership of the Common Market" and was concerned to resolve any problems that might have been caused by the accession of the United Kingdom.[26] Is it possible that he contemplated the introduction of the two principles in order that English law would be better prepared for the challenges ahead? If so, then Lord Diplock could have sought to pre-empt the influence of European principles by their active adoption into English law prior to the increasing influence of Community law.[27] Alternatively, Lord Diplock could merely have wished to change the language of review to a more European style. In the words of Sir William Wade:[28]

> "[Lord Diplock's] . . . opinion, as I believe, was that proportionality and legitimate expectation were different more in name than in substance from the English rules, though he realised that it might be necessary for British judges to adopt them as the influence of European law became ever more insistent."

However, the fact that Lord Diplock considered the adoption of the principles suggests that he did not view the change merely to be one of language, but also one of principle.

Finally, it is possible to interpret Lord Diplock's interest in adopting these principles as another means by which the judiciary, with the value of their political experience gained through the common law tradition, could supervise the decisions of administrative bodies. Viewed in this way, the adoption of the principles would allow an alternative means by which traditional English judicial values could be articulated against executive incursions on liberty, albeit in a more conceptually precise method than the ordinary common law rules; in which case the principles would have been viewed as fitting into the common law tradition of continuity and innovation. Rather than fearing that the European principles would "imperil the heritage of the Common Law",[29] Lord Diplock could have considered using them as a means of protecting that heritage.

It is submitted that Lord Diplock was influenced to some extent by all of these intentions. The adoption of legitimate expectations and proportionality would keep English law up to date with European developments and enhance the development of domestic administrative law. Membership of the European Community and the need for British judges to apply the principles as a matter of Community law created an impetus to adopt them prior to the direct influence of Community law. Furthermore, by seeking to introduce new principles, Lord Diplock could have viewed himself as exemplifying the attitude of those

---

[26] Lord Diplock, above at n. 22, 3.

[27] See the comment of Lord Roskill quoted in the text below at n. 42, which supports this view.

[28] Letter from Sir William Wade to the author dated 26 March 1997. Wade has long held the view that problems in administrative law stem from a confusion of terminology or verbal misunderstandings: see H.W.R. Wade, "'Quasi-judicial' and its Background" (1949) 10 *CLJ* 216, 218; H.W.R. Wade, "The Twilight of Natural Justice?" (1951) 67 *LQR* 103, 109.

[29] Lord Diplock, above at n. 22, 4.

bold nineteenth century judges he so admired.[30] Although he did not articulate these intentions, they could not have been far from his mind. Pulling together the various strands, it is clear that Lord Diplock's project was a conscious attempt to integrate the principles into English law.

Of course, this is not to imply that other lawyers necessarily agreed with this project. For instance, Wade questioned whether English law needed to import new principles since the doctrine of reasonableness would allow British judges to react against any element of unfairness, whether procedural or substantive.[31] In the opinion of Lord Wilberforce, the European Court only operated in a narrow field and was "not a court which develops doctrines or jurisprudential theories which have any impact on English law".[32] However, for a Law Lord who openly admitted that courts on occasion needed to legislate[33] and who had achieved an "almost Olympian"[34] predominance in the House of Lords, such concerns could be put aside. Furthermore, Lord Diplock's "quality of persuading his colleagues . . . [which] . . . almost got to the stage of a mesmeric quality" and his "intellectual superiority, coupled with enormous hard work" may have enabled him to persuade his colleagues to accept his point of view.[35] Lord Diplock would also have been able to point to the use of the same language by Lord Denning in the Court of Appeal.[36] It is clear that Lord Diplock marked out the path others were subsequently to tread.

It was not until 1984, in the *GCHQ* case, that Lord Diplock gave a comprehensive statement on judicial review.[37] According to Lord Scarman, this speech was "in a very real sense a last testament".[38] It is worth focusing upon this statement for the following reasons. First, Lord Diplock suggested a novel categorisation of judicial review under the three heads of illegality, irrationality and procedural impropriety. This tripartite classification was a product of the rationalisation of judicial review prompted in part by the huge increase in the numbers of applications during the 1980s. Questions of *vires* and jurisdiction were to be replaced with simple questions of legality. Unreasonableness was redefined from the tautological definition provided by Lord Greene MR[39] to irrationality. The Latin tags *audi alteram partem* and *nemo judex in causa sua* were to be assimilated under a general ground of procedural impropriety.

---

[30] See Sir Kenneth Diplock, *The Courts as Legislators* (Holdsworth Club, University of Birmingham, 1965).

[31] H.W.R. Wade, *Constitutional Fundamentals* (Stevens, London, revised ed. 1989), 95.

[32] Lord Wilberforce, interviewed in G. Sturgess and P. Chubb (eds), *Judging the World: Law and Politics in the World's Leading Courts* (Butterworths, London, 1988), 271, 276.

[33] See Lord Diplock, *The Courts as Legislators*, above at n. 30.

[34] "Influential Law Lord", *The Times,* 16 October 1985, 18.

[35] Lord Wilberforce, in Sturgess and Chubb, above at n. 32, 275.

[36] See the *Schmidt* and *Hook* cases, above at n. 3.

[37] *Council of Civil Service Unions* v. *Minister for the Civil Service* [1985] AC 374.

[38] Lord Scarman, "The Development of Administrative Law: Obstacles and Opportunities" [1990] *PL* 490. The speeches in the *GCHQ* case were delivered on 22 November 1984. Lord Diplock died on 14 October 1985. See P.V. Baker, "Lord Diplock 1907–1985" (1986) 102 *LQR* 1.

[39] *Associated Provincial Picture Houses Ltd.* v. *Wednesbury Corporation* [1948] 1 KB 223.

Secondly, Lord Diplock also used his speech to mark the possible future direction of the law. It therefore contained an exposition of the principle of legitimate expectations as it had developed until then. Lord Diplock also remarked that in articulating the heads of review he had in mind:[40]

"particularly the possible adoption in the future of the principle of 'proportionality' which is recognised in the administrative law of several of our fellow members of the European Economic Community."

The influence of the general principles of European law is evident. In the words of Lord Mackenzie Stuart:[41]

"[t]he concept of recognising that a failure to respect legitimate expectations may give rise, in public law, to a remedy is a novelty in English law and lacks discernible English parentage. To find the true ancestry one does not have to look far across the Channel."

Lord Roskill has intimated that in referring to the possible adoption of proportionality Lord Diplock:[42]

"clearly had in mind the likely increasing influence of Community law upon our domestic law which might in time lead to the further adoption of this principle as a separate category and not merely as a possible reinforcement of one or more of these stated categories such as irrationality."

In this, his last exposition on judicial review, Lord Diplock celebrated the advances made over the previous thirty years, classified the heads of challenge as principles of public law, endorsed the principle of legitimate expectations and advanced the possible adoption of proportionality. By giving this magisterial speech, Lord Diplock was seeking to ensure that judicial review, or rather his own articulation of it,[43] became firmly entrenched in English law and could be developed by future judges. His approach was that the judges should develop the law in a way that is responsive to social needs. He therefore led the judicial movement for the development of administrative law within the sphere of common law. For Lord Diplock there was now a system of administrative law in England merely as a result of a few landmark cases[44] and procedural innovations. However, this underestimated the complexity of the problems involved in developing a system of administrative law and of assimilating Continental principles within it. How could common law judges, educated in the tradition that government is subject to the ordinary law of the land, accommodate two principles predicated on the assumption that public law is a distinct form of legal

---

[40] *GCHQ*, above at n. 37, 410E.

[41] Lord Mackenzie Stuart, "Recent Developments in English Administrative Law—The Impact of Europe?", in F. Capotorti (ed.), *Du droit international au droit de l'integration: Liber Amicorum Pierre Pescatore* (Nomos Verlagsgesellschaft, Baden-Baden, 1987), 411, 417.

[42] *R. v. Secretary of State for the Home Department, ex parte Brind* [1991] 1 AC 696, 750D.

[43] See, e.g., *R. v. Panel on Takeovers and Mergers, ex parte Datafin plc* [1987] QB 815, 836H, *per* Lord Donaldson MR; H.W.R. Wade, *Administrative Law* (Clarendon Press, Oxford, 6th ed. 1988), viii; Lord Wilberforce, in Sturgess and Chubb, above at n. 32.

[44] See *Ridge*, above at n. 1; *Padfield*, above at n. 7; *Anisminic*, above at n. 7.

discourse? Do English judges possess sufficient knowledge of administrative processes to apply these principles effectively? Should the courts have a wider scope to make findings of fact? These and other important questions were never raised by Lord Diplock or other judges.

In conclusion, Lord Diplock should be viewed as having exerted a powerful influence in identifying the agenda for English judicial review. His eminent standing ensured that the language of "public law", "proportionality" and "legitimate expectations" gained a firm foothold in the vocabulary of English law. However, while Lord Diplock succeeded in introducing this new language, ironically he could exercise little influence over the subsequent conceptual development of the principles. That task inevitably passed to other judges who may not have shared Lord Diplock's views or even recognised the principles to be of Continental origin. This is not to deny that other judges have subsequently endorsed his project. Speaking some twenty years after Lord Diplock first advanced the idea of assimilating the principles, Lord Goff recognised the beneficial influence of European law on English law. His Lordship remarked that this trade in ideas "must surely be regarded as fruitful. While never letting our critical guard down, we should welcome rather than reject these new ideas".[45] Sir Thomas Bingham has also noted the European parentage of the principles, and intimated that "it would be worth a modest investment in proportionality as a growth stock".[46] However, other judges have experienced disorientation and even irritation when bringing their minds to bear upon the principles.[47]

THE CHALLENGE OF COMMUNITY LAW

A century after Dicey rejected *droit administratif* as incompatible with the rule of law,[48] the English courts are facing the challenge presented by the Community rule of law. For the purposes of the European Court of Justice the rule of law enforces the general principles of law which are derived from Continental systems of administrative law. Since the entry of the United Kingdom into the European Community, the "new legal order"[49] has posed major challenges for the British constitution. For instance, the question of the compatibility of the supremacy of Community law with the sovereignty of Parliament,[50] the obligation to interpret national laws in conformity with

---

[45] Lord Goff of Chieveley, "The Future of the Common Law" (1997) 46 *ICLQ* 745, 747.

[46] Sir Thomas Bingham, "'There is a World Elsewhere': The Changing Perspectives of English Law" (1992) 41 *ICLQ* 513, 524.

[47] See, e.g., *Brind*, above at n. 42; *R. v. Secretary of State for the Home Department, ex parte Hargreaves* [1997] 1 All ER 397.

[48] A.V. Dicey, *An Introduction to the Study of the Law of the Constitution* (Macmillan, London, 10th ed. 1959), ch. XII.

[49] Case 26/62 *Van Gend en Loos v. Nederlandse Administratie der Belastingen* [1963] ECR 1, 12.

[50] *R. v. Secretary of State for Transport, ex parte Factortame Ltd. (No. 2)* [1991] 1 AC 603.

European directives,[51] the need to identify which bodies provide "a public service under the control of the State" and have special powers for that purpose[52] in order to allow individuals to rely on the vertical direct effect of directives, the right to an effective remedy,[53] the liability of the State for breach of Community law[54] and the differential standards of legality for reviewing administrative action, have formed the issues through which the challenge of Community law has emerged.

Community law exerts an external pressure on English administrative law that will become more acute with the development of the Community and legal challenges brought before English courts. It is not simply the extent of the encroachment of actual Community laws which is having an impact on English law, but rather the philosophy and style underpinning Community law. The European jurisprudence is based on a different philosophy of law, government and the individual than that of English law, and the rational and more principled approach typical of Continental legal styles clashes with the traditional pragmatic common law method.[55] In other words, the difference between the more purposive orientation of Continental administrative law and the common law is no longer of mere comparative interest, but forms a central issue concerning the effectiveness of Community law in the United Kingdom. The challenge presented by Community law should be viewed as an essentially cultural challenge to the distinctive nature of the common law method.

The first public lawyer to identify this unintended consequence of British membership was J.D.B. Mitchell,[56] who recognised that as public power was no longer being contained at the national level but was being extended to the European Community, the issue of law in relation to the exercise of that power would arise. As English law has a very distinct approach to law and government, the exercise of power at the Community presented problems for English law since it would have to accommodate the influence of Community law which, being drawn from the Continental tradition, differed substantially from the English approach. Mitchell's argument was that English ways of considering law and public power would have to be modernised in order to meet the challenge presented by Community law. For example, the doctrine of Parliamentary

---

[51] Case 14/83 *Von Colson and Kamann* v. *Land Nordrhein-Westfalen* [1984] ECR 1891; Case C–106/89 *Marleasing SA* v. *La Comercial Internacionale de Alimentacion SA* [1990] ECR I–4135. See also *Duke v. Reliance Systems Ltd*. [1988] AC 618.

[52] Case C–188/89 *Foster* v. *British Gas* [1990] ECR I–3133, para. 22. See also *Doughty* v. *Rolls Royce plc* [1992] 1 CMLR 1045.

[53] *Factortame (No. 2)*, above at n. 50.

[54] Joined Cases C–6 and 9/90 *Francovich* v. *Italy* [1991] ECR I–5357; Joined Cases C–46 and 48/93 *Brasserie du Pêcheur SA* v. *Germany*, R. v. *Secretary of State for Transport, ex parte Factortame Ltd. (No. 3)* [1996] ECR I–1029. See also *Bourgoin SA* v. *Ministry of Agriculture, Fisheries and Food* [1986] QB 716.

[55] See the House of Lords European Communities Committee, *Special Report* (Session 1974–75) H.L. 38; J. Temple Lang, "The Constitutional Principles Governing Community Legislation" (1989) 40 *NILQ* 227, 242–5.

[56] See, generally, M. Loughlin, "Sitting on a Fence at Carter Bar: In Praise of J.D.B. Mitchell" (1991) 36 *Juridical Review* 135.

sovereignty had to be developed in light of changing circumstances, such as accession to the European Community.[57] In 1969 Mitchell observed that "there is emerging a new order of European public law between traditional international law and domestic law . . . [which] . . . means that terms such as 'Administrative/constitutional' must in this larger context be re-interpreted".[58] Mitchell was concerned that English law should be able to meet the challenge posed by the external influence of Community law. His conclusion was that English lawyers should think in terms of a system of public law which was both purposive and susceptible.[59] Public law should be purposive in that it focuses on the objectives sought to be achieved by the administration and would therefore be less technical and more creative. The counterpart to this was a "susceptibility of lawyers in understanding the realities and problems of the governmental process".[60] Mitchell argued that "[t]here is no reason why rational constructive thought should not be brought to bear on government" and, as experiment was impossible, "[t]he only substitute . . . can be the comparative method pursued in depth".[61] However, "[s]uperficiality remains a real danger which is enhanced by facile but misleading translation of terms".[62] Underpinning this functionalist approach is a view of law as a part of the apparatus of government, as opposed to Dicey's view of law as an autonomous, analytical discipline. Mitchell would then have argued that lawyers should seek means of dealing constructively with both the efficient achievement of governmental objectives and the fair treatment of individuals. The interpretation of English law in the light of the new, emerging European public law could therefore help to achieve this purposive orientation.

If the central issue facing English law since the use of legislation on a large scale for social purposes has been to develop a conception of legality appropriate to the developing system of governance, then the challenge of Community law brings this issue into sharper focus by highlighting the differential approaches to the role of law in government. Other European States have experienced a similar socialisation of the law, and their legal systems have sought to deal with the issues arising from this constructively, which, in turn, has influenced Community law.

Having identified the general nature of the challenge presented by European law this section will now focus upon the issue of the differentiation between

---

[57] J.D.B. Mitchell, "The Sovereignty of Parliament and Community Law: The Stumbling-Block That Isn't There" (1979) 55 *International Affairs* 33; J.D.B. Mitchell, "What Happened to the Constitution on 1st January 1973?" (1980) 11 *Cambrian LR* 69.

[58] J.D.B. Mitchell, "Why European Institutions?", in J.D.B. Mitchell and L.J. Brinkhorst, *European Law and Institutions* (Edinburgh University Press, Edinburgh, 1969), 30, 41.

[59] J.D.B. Mitchell, "Administrative Law and Policy Effectiveness", in J.A.G. Griffith (ed.), *From Policy to Administration: Essays in Honour of William A Robson* (Allen & Unwin, London, 1976), 174, 193.

[60] Mitchell, above at n. 58, 44.

[61] Ibid., 49–50.

[62] Ibid., 50.

English and Community law of legal standards placed upon public administration. In fulfilling their obligation to give effective legal protection to Community law rights,[63] English courts have realised that they are compelled to provide greater legal protection under Community law than is usually the case under English law. Differential standards of legality apply and are determined by whether an applicant's case falls within the scope of either Community or domestic law. For instance, if an individual seeks to rely on a treaty right, such as the free movement of workers, which has direct effect, then the national court will have to determine whether that right has been infringed by reference to European principles.[64] General principles will also fall to be applied to action by a Member State required by Community law.[65] Much Community administration is indirect; Community institutions exercise policy-making powers but the implementation and enforcement of schemes, such as the Common Agricultural Policy, is devolved to national bodies. Not only are European programs of regulation more juridified and legalistic than the typically, more discretionary-based British style of regulation,[66] but the exercise of such powers will require national courts to apply general principles of Community law since the source of the power stems from Community law. National courts, as well as national administrators, have found themselves involved in the process of ensuring the effective implementation and application of Community law. The upshot of this has been the emergence of a strange dichotomy in legal protection whereby the legal standards to which an individual is entitled can differ depending upon whether his case is brought through either domestic or Community law. In the words of Laws J.:[67]

> "*Wednesbury* and European review are different models—one looser, one tighter—of the same juridical concept, which is the imposition of compulsory standards on decision-makers so as to secure the repudiation of arbitrary power."

The Government itself has recognised that "European Community law has provided new rights and expectations, some of which may only be vindicated within the context of judicial review".[68] As Community law draws the boundaries of legality more tightly than English law there may be considerable pres-

---

[63] See, generally, F. Snyder, "The Effectiveness of European Community Law: Institutions, Processes, Tools and Techniques" (1993) 56 *MLR* 19.

[64] On direct effect, see P.P. Craig and G. de Búrca, *EU Law: Text, Cases and Materials* (Clarendon Press, Oxford, 2nd ed. 1998), ch. 4.

[65] *R. v. Ministry of Agriculture, Fisheries and Food, ex parte First City Trading Ltd.* [1997] 1 CMLR 250, 268–9. See also J. Temple Lang, "The Sphere in Which Member States are Obliged to Comply with the General Principles of Law and Community Fundamental Rights Principles" [1991/2] *Legal Issues of European Integration* 23.

[66] See T. Daintith (ed), *Implementing EC Law in the United Kingdom: Structures For Indirect Rule* (Wiley, Chichester, 1995); A. Hunt, "Regulation of Telecommunications: the Developing EU Regulatory Framework and its Impact on the United Kingdom" (1997) 3 *EPL* 93.

[67] *First City Trading Ltd.*, above at n. 65, 279.

[68] Government evidence to the Treasury and Civil Service Select Committee, 26 April 1994, quoted in A. Marr, *Ruling Britannia: The Failure and Future of British Democracy* (Penguin, Harmondsworth, 1996), 288.

sure to provide the same standard of legal protection under domestic law as is required by Community law for the following reasons.

First, the method of interpretation which the European Court draws from comparative law acts as a powerful lever for the interpenetration and reconciliation of the national laws of the Member States.[69] The European Court adopts the most progressive principles from the national law of the Member States in order to develop the general principles of Community law. If the European Court has adopted a principle from a national legal order this may lead to an evaluation of how such principles compete with the law of other Member States. As Community law imposes more constraints on the exercise of public power it raises the question of whether it is more successful in the avoidance of arbitrariness than English law. As Sir Gordon Slynn has commented, if the general principles of law "are applied in a Community law context, it seems not improbable that they will have their effect on decisions in an analogous context under domestic law".[70] Related to this is the fact that the Community can act as a forum for seeking common solutions to common problems.[71] Since "Community law . . . derives from not only the economic but also the legal interpenetration of the Member States"[72] it can act as a means of resolving common national problems through shared Community solutions. For example, Lord Diplock, as part of his quest to determine how the courts should control administrative power, came to acknowledge the principles by attending conferences on European administrative law. From a functionalist perspective, Mitchell, who had consistently argued that England lacked a distinct system of public law, was optimistic about the possible reformative effects of the "richness" of Community law on English law: "[t]here is an excitement about ideas even if couched in arid terms like 'proportionality', or 'legitimate expectation' . . . which invigorates debate, and the debate then corresponds to current reality".[73]

Secondly, the application of Community law by national courts highlights areas of national law where a different approach is adopted. The obligation on English courts to apply Community law has required judges to adopt a new constitutional role in examining the legality of primary legislation and a more intensive approach to judicial review. One consequence of this new judicial approach under Community law is that it has uncovered areas of national law where a lesser degree of legal protection is offered, which results in inconsistent legal protection for individuals. This creates a corresponding pressure to modify national law to avoid any inconsistency. For example, in *In Re M*[74] the House

---

[69] Y. Galmot, "*Réflexions sur le recours au droit comparé par la Cour de Justice des Communautés européenes*" (1990) 6 *Revue français droit administratif* 255, 261.

[70] G. Slynn, "But in England there is no . . . ", in W. Fuerst (ed.), *Festschrift für Wolfgang Zeidler Volume 1* (Berlin/New York, 1987), 397, 400.

[71] T. Koopmans, "European Public Law: Reality and Prospects" [1991] *PL* 53, 54.

[72] Case 155/79 *AM & S Europe Ltd. v. Commission* [1982] ECR 1575, para. 18.

[73] Mitchell, above at n. 57, 45–6.

[74] [1994] 1 AC 377.

of Lords reconsidered the rule that interim injunctions were not available against the Crown following the *Factortame*[75] case where the European Court had held that Community law required the possibility that such injunctions could be granted. Lord Woolf stated that "it would be most regrettable if an approach which is inconsistent with that which exists in Community law should be allowed to persist if . . . [it] . . . was not strictly necessary".[76] Community law required a remedy which English law did not provide. The result was that English law provided less legal protection than Community law and therefore created an unjust dichotomy by not treating like cases alike.[77] The House of Lords resolved this problem by reconsidering the rule.

In Re M demonstrates that English courts need to be aware of the level of legal protection provided under Community law, and attempt to reconcile English and Community law in cases of inconsistency, or risk the development of a two-speed system of guarantees for litigants. Sedley J., as he then was, has recognised that as the standards of the European Convention of Human Rights inform the jurisprudence of the European Court of Justice, it would be "unreal and poten-tially unjust to continue to develop English public law without reference to them".[78] The potential inequality arising from such differences would appear to be just as great in relation to the general principles of Community law. Such judicial concerns are in part a reflection of the profound changes in public power. As administrative power is no longer a self-contained national phenom-enon; administrative law concerning the exercise of such powers can similarly be no longer self-contained. This Europeanisation of administrative power and law must inevitably have an impact on national legal systems. For instance, there is no obligation for an English judge deciding a domestic case to apply pro-portionality. Neverthless, Lord Slynn has noted that it might "creep in", partic-ularly when Community law and domestic law issues coincide or overlap:[79]

> "When a judge in the same case is going to have to decide national law and Community law issues, it is almost too much to ask that he should try to keep *Wednesbury* unreasonableness for one, proportionality for the other. It may even be undesirable that he should try to do so."

When English courts are required to apply the general principles of Community law, which find no equivalent in English law, the disparity will be

---

[75] *Factortame (No. 2)*, above at n. 50.

[76] *In Re M*, above at n. 74, 422G. Cf. H. Woolf, "Judicial Review: A Possible Programme For Reform" [1992] *PL* 221, 233. See also *Woolwich Building Society v. Inland Revenue Commissioners* [1993] AC 70, 177E, *per* Lord Goff; *R. v. Secretary of State for Transport, ex parte Factortame* [1998] 3 CMLR 192, 207; Law Commission Consultation Paper No. 126, *Administrative Law: Judicial Review and Statutory Appeals* (HMSO, London, 1993), para. 2.10.

[77] See I. Ward, "Fairness, Effectiveness and Fundamental Rights: The Case For a Unified Administrative Law Within the European Community" (1994) 5 *Touro International LR* 279.

[78] *R. v. Secretary of State for the Home Department, ex parte McQuillan* [1995] 4 All ER 400, 422h.

[79] Lord Slynn, "European Law and the National Judge", in *Butterworth Lectures 1991–92* (Butterworths, London, 1993), 18, 27–8.

more evident and the potential injustice for the individual will be great. The inconsistency in legal protection may be more apparent in English law than in other Member States where a higher level of legal protection is guaranteed or where a constitutional provision of equality would prevent such inconsistent legal protection. If English law does not recognise any substantive restraint on discretionary power other than that of *Wednesbury* unreasonableness, it is unrealistic to hope that this ground will provide protection equal to that afforded by the general principles of Community law.[80] Again, as early as the mid-1970s Mitchell that "[a] reconciliation of concepts becomes essential if the individual is not to suffer".[81] More recently, Walter van Gerven has proposed that in order to prevent an undesirable drifting apart of Community and national rules governing similar situations a principle of homogeneity must be introduced in order to keep the two sets of rules together.[82] Furthermore, there seems to be a growing awareness among the English judiciary of the influence of Community law and the need to maintain a consistent approach. Neill L.J. has intimated that "there is much to be said for the view that all the courts in the European Community should apply common standards in the field of administrative law".[83]

Such pressures may create an osmotic or "spill-over" effect of European law, whereby principles which need only be applied by the national court when it is concerned with Community law may nevertheless filter through into the court's elaboration of domestic law. As a result of such "osmotic reciprocal influence"[84] between Community and national law and the development towards a model of European public administration,[85] it has been argued that a common European administrative law is now developing.[86] However, while the impact of Community law is potentially profound, its actual influence will be uneven. The infection of legal concepts tends to depend upon immediate exposure to a source.[87] This sort of infection does not include general issues such as the

---

[80] See, e.g., *R. v. Secretary of State for the Home Department, ex parte Adams* [1995] All ER (EC) 177.

[81] Mitchell, above at n. 59, 192.

[82] W. van Gerven, "Bridging the Gap Between Community and National Laws: Towards a Principle of Homogeneity in the Field of Legal Remedies?" (1995) 32 *CML Rev.* 679, 699–702.

[83] *R. v. Secretary of State for the Environment, ex parte National and Local Government Officers' Association* [1993] 5 Admin. LR 785, 800G.

[84] G. Ress, quoted in G.F. Schuppert, "On the Evolution of a European State: Reflections on the Conditions of and Prospects for a European Constitution", in J.J. Hesse and N. Johnson (eds), *Constitutional Policy and Change in Europe* (Oxford University Press, Oxford, 1995), 329, 349–50.

[85] See, e.g., S. Cassese, "Towards a European Model of Public Administration", in D.S. Clark (ed.), *Comparative and Private International Law: Essays in Honour of John Henry Merryman on his Seventieth Birthday* (Berlin, 1990), 353. See also Y. Mény, P. Muller and J.-L. Quermonne, *Adjusting to Europe: the impact of the European Union on national institutions and policies* (Routledge, London, 1996).

[86] See J. Rivero, "*Vers un Droit Commun Européen: Nouvelles Perspectives en Droit Administratif*", in M. Cappelletti (ed.), *New Perspectives For a Common Law of Europe* (Sijthoff, Leyden, 1978), 389; J. Schwarze, *European Administrative Law* (Sweet & Maxwell, London, 1992); J. Schwarze (ed.), *Administrative Law under European Influence: On the Convergence of the Administrative Laws of the EU Member States* (Sweet & Maxwell, London, 1996).

[87] Cf. *Factortame (No. 2)*, above at n. 50; and *In Re M*, above at n. 74.

doctrinal or theoretical underpinning of Continental administrative law. In the absence of consideration of such wider issues, English judges exposed to Community law may attempt to "patch-up" English law to attain equality of protection for individuals. However, precisely because such wider issues are not considered, English courts may be unable to integrate the European jurisprudence effectively. The danger is that the courts will view English law as providing equality of protection because it has changed its conceptual language into European terminology. In order that the common law is able to respond effectively to the challenge of Community law, English courts will need to avoid this specious remedy and instead seek an understanding of law appropriate to meeting the challenge. National approaches to law and administration reflect different styles, methods and cultural attitudes, which may constitute strong forces against the convergence of administrative law. Classifications such as private law and public law are fundamental to ways of thinking. This difference of approach is particularly pronounced between the English and Continental traditions of administrative law.

The emergence of European administrative law has created pressures for convergence between English and Continental administrative law. However, equally strong pressures for divergence exist. Since Community law is predicated upon a different philosophy of law and government to English law, this will create tensions simultaneously both for and against the convergence of administrative law. The common law may experience the influx of new principles providing greater protection for individuals and, therefore, be under pressure to "level up". However, precisely because this difference in legal protection is predicated upon a different underlying philosophy to law and government, common law may be unable to meet the challenge presented by Community law. Finally, it may be noted that there will be no escape from the external pressure of Community law on English administrative law, apart from the unlikely prospect of the United Kingdom withdrawing altogether from the European Union.

This chapter has examined the different forces behind the integration of principles in English law. It has been seen that pressures have come both from within and outside the English legal system. The purpose of the following chapters is to compare the elaboration of the principles in English and European law against the different traditions of administrative law.

3

Legitimate Expectations

THE PRINCIPLE OF legitimate expectations concerns the relationship between public administration and the individual. It seeks to resolve the basic conflict between the desire to protect the individual's confidence in expectations raised by administrative conduct and the need for administrators to pursue changing policy objectives. The principle means that expectations raised as a result of administrative conduct may have legal consequences. Either the administration must respect those expectations or provide compelling reasons why the public interest must take priority. The principle therefore concerns the degree to which an individual's expectations may be safeguarded in the face of a change of policy which tends to undermine them. The role of the administrative court is to determine the extent to which the individual's expectation can be accommodated within changing policy objectives.

The purpose of this chapter is to compare the principle of legitimate expectations in European Community law and English law. It will examine the contrast between judicial attitudes towards, and the different meanings attributed to, "legitimate expectation" in the two legal systems. Since both the European Court of Justice and the English courts have developed the principle over a similar period of time this comparison will be instructive.[1] The structure of this chapter will be as follows: the development of the principle in European and English law; and a comparison of specific aspects of the principle.

LEGITIMATE EXPECTATIONS IN EUROPEAN COMMUNITY LAW

The European Court of Justice has integrated legitimate expectations into its review of legality since the 1970s and recognises that it "forms part of the Community legal order".[2] The development of the principle was inspired by

---

[1] English courts have not been alone in developing legitimate expectations as part of their national law. See the decision of the Strasbourg Administrative Court in *Entreprise Freymuth* c. *Ministre de l'Environnement*, 8 December 1994 [1995] *Actualité Juridique: Droit Administratif 555* (conclusions of the *commissaire du gouvernement*); noted by R. Errera [1995] *PL* 657.

[2] Case 112/77 *August Töpfer & Co. GmbH* v. *Commission* [1978] ECR 1019, para. 19. For overviews of the European Court's case law, see F. Hubeau, "*Le principe de la protection de la confiance legitime dans la jurisprudence de la cour de justice des communautes europeennes*" (1983) 19 *Cahiers de Droit Européen* 143; K.-D. Borchardt, "*Vertrauensschutz im Europäischen Gemeinschaftsrecht: Die Rechtsprechung des EuGH von Algera über CNTA bis Mulder und von Deetzen*" (1988) 15 *Europäische Grundrechte Zeitschrift* 309; E. Sharpston, "European Community Law and the Doctrine of Legitimate Expectations: How Legitimate, and For Whom?" (1990) 11

the German principle of *vertrauensschutz,* meaning the protection of trust.[3] For example, in the *Westzucker* case the Finance Court of Hesse requested a preliminary reference from the European Court asking whether a regulation infringed "a principle of legal certainty by which the confidence of persons concerned deserves to be protected (*Vertrauensschutz*)".[4] Advocate-General Roemer stated that the issue of a licence could create an expectation which, if the administration changed the situation, would be disappointed, thereby creating a loss for the individual. Referring to a decision of the Federal Constitutional Court (*Bundesverfassungsgericht*) the Advocate-General stated that the change of situation requires a "weighing up of respective interests" since any interference with an individual's expectations could "only be sanctioned if public interests predominate".[5] Presumably, the European Court considered legitimate expectations to be a progressive and carefully considered principle. The European Court has also recognised the need to provide equivalent protection to that of the best performing national legal systems.[6] It is probable that this was also a reason for the adoption of the principle.[7]

What this chapter will endeavour to demonstrate is that the European Court uses legitimate expectations to enforce a minimal standard of treatment for individuals without defeating the public interest objectives in administration. The task of modern administrative law is to ensure that public programmes are carried out both equitably and effectively. To achieve this the administrative court adapts its review towards the purposes for which public power is exercised.[8] The principle of legitimate expectations is used to ensure that the administration achieves its objectives while, so far as possible, protecting the individual's expectations. By using law as a means of administration a balance is achieved between the public interest and the individual's expectations. The Court contributes towards Community policy by ensuring that the administration is able to achieve its objectives, but also guards against over-zealous policy implemen-

---

Northwestern Journal of International Law and Business 87; J. Schwarze, *European Administrative Law* (Sweet & Maxwell, London, 1992), ch. 6. For an economic analysis see, E. Sharpston, "Legitimate Expectations and Economic Reality" (1990) 15 *ELRev* 103.

[3] See F. Ossenbühl, "*Vertrauensschutz im sozialen Rechtsstaat*" (1972) 25 *Die Öffentliche Verwaltung* 25; G. Nolte, "General Principles of German and European Administrative Law—A Comparison in Historical Perspective" (1994) 57 *MLR* 191, 195, 203.

[4] Case 1/73 *Westzucker GmbH* v. *Einfuhr- und Vorratsstelle für Zucker* [1973] ECR 723, para. 6. See also Case 81/72 *Commission* v. *Council* [1973] ECR 575.

[5] Ibid., 741 (col. 1). Cf. the decision of the German Federal Constitutional Court of 23 March 1971 (1971) 24 *Die Öffentliche Verwaltung* 605.

[6] See, e.g., Case 14/61 *Koninklijke Nederlandsche Hoogovens en Staalfabrieken NV* v. *High Authority of the European Coal and Steel Community* [1962] ECR 253, 279 of Advocate-General Lagrange's opinion; Case C–49/88 *Al-Jubail Fertilizer Company and Saudi Arabian Fertilizer Company* v. *Commission* [1991] ECR I–3187, para. 16.

[7] It may be noted that German law requires the protection of some expectations that the European Court would consider impairs the efficiency of Community law. See Case C–5/89 *Commission* v. *Germany* [1990] ECR I–3437; Case 2–24/95 *Land Rheinland-Pfalz* v. *Alcan Deutschland GmbH* [1997] ECR I–1591.

[8] See E. Schmidt-Aßmann, "Basic Principles of German Administrative Law" (1993) 35 *Journal of the Indian Law Institute* 65.

tation that can create injustice for individuals. In doing so the European Court enhances the acceptability and legitimacy of the Community administration.

An illustration of legitimate expectations is provided by the *Mulder* case.[9] This litigation involved a dispute over the scheme of milk production in the Community. For many years the milk market had suffered from over-supply.[10] In 1977 the European Council adopted measures to regulate this sector and solve the surplus problem. One regulation aimed at encouraging milk producers to cease production for a period of time.[11] If a producer made an undertaking to suspend production for five years it would be awarded a non-marketing premium. A further regulation introduced a "co-responsibility levy" for all milk processing.[12]

Several milk producers, including the applicant, agreed to suspend production. However, this did not solve the surplus problem and the Council adopted more stringent measures in 1984.[13] A regulation was introduced imposing a "super-levy" on top of the "co-responsibility levy".[14] This levy was payable where milk deliveries exceeded a given "reference quantity" which was calculated on the basis of milk production in a previous year (the "reference year").[15]

The applicant was a Dutch farmer who had made an undertaking in 1979 to cease milk production for five years. Towards the end of this period he intended to resume production and applied for a reference quantity. However, this was refused because he did not produce any milk in the reference year, 1983. Without a reference quantity he would be charged the super-levy for his milk production. He had missed out on a reference quantity because he had suspended production following the non-marketing undertaking. The applicant claimed that the reference quantity scheme violated his legitimate expectations. The European Court reasoned that a producer who had given up and later resumed milk production could not expect to do so under exactly the same market conditions as existed when they had ceased production. It was not legitimate to expect that such producers would not be subject to any market or structural policy introduced in the meantime. However, the applicant could legitimately expect to be able to resume production without being restricted from doing so precisely because he had been encouraged to suspend his milk production:[16]

"The fact remains that where such a producer, as in the present case, has been encouraged by a Community measure to suspend marketing for a limited period in the

---

[9] Case 120/86 *Mulder* v. *Minister van Laudbouw en Visserij* [1988] ECR 2321. See also Case 170/86 *Von Deetzen* v. *Hauptzollamt Hamburg-Jonas* [1988] ECR 2355.

[10] See M. Cardwell, *Milk Quotas: European Community and United Kingdom Law* (Clarendon Press, Oxford, 1996), 5–8.

[11] Regulation No. 1078/77 (OJ 1977 L131/1).

[12] Regulation No. 1079/77 (OJ 1977 L131/6).

[13] For more detail, see G, Avery, "The Common Agricultural Policy: a Turning Point?" (1984) 21 *CML Rev.* 481; Cardwell, above at n. 10, 11–23.

[14] Regulation No. 856/84 (OJ 1984 L90/10).

[15] Regulation No. 857/84 (OJ 1984 L90/13).

[16] *Mulder*, above at n. 9, para. 24.

general interest and against payment of a premium he may legitimately expect not to be subject, upon expiry of his undertaking, to restrictions which specifically affect him precisely because he availed himself of the possibilities offered by the Community provisions."

The applicant had been effectively excluded from marketing milk because he had made the non-marketing undertaking. When he agreed to suspend production in 1979 it was unforeseeable that he would not be awarded a reference quantity since the system was not introduced until 1984. The Court invalidated the regulation as it breached the producer's legitimate expectations. The expectation was that the ability of the producer to resume production would not be restricted because he had made the undertaking. The European Court stressed that it was not possible to rely upon legitimate expectations for normal trading losses. As Advocate-General Slynn noted, the court was concerned that the individual did suffer from "unreasonable treatment" by the Community, as opposed to the "hard business luck" which a producer could expect to risk in the market.[17]

The case demonstrates the European Court's concern that policy objectives are implemented fairly and equitably. The Community had put the producers in a special position because of the undertaking not to produce milk. In implementing a new policy initiative the Community institutions had to take account of the expectations of those producers. By upholding the applicant's legitimate expectations the European Court was not seeking to defeat the change in policy but to secure, as far as possible, the special position of producers who had made the undertaking.

While the European Court has not itself provided any theoretical justification for the protection of legitimate expectations, various justifications have been advanced. Advocate-General Trabucchi remarked that the principle "has a specific equitable function"[18] which ensured "fair dealing and good faith"[19] as minimal standards of Community administration. It would be unfair for the administration to raise certain expectations as to its future conduct which are then subsequently disappointed, without good reason. The principle enables the European Court to achieve a "balance between equity and the rigour of law".[20] For Jürgen Schwarze the principle is merely a general maxim derived from the notion that the Community is based upon the rule of law.[21] In order that individuals can arrange their lives the law needs to be certain, regular and pre-

---

[17] Ibid., 2341 (col. 2).

[18] Case 5/75 *Deuka, Deutsche Kraftfutter GmbH BJ Stolp* v. *Einfuhr- und Vorratsstelle für Getreide und Futtermittel* [1975] ECR 759, 777 (col. 2) of the Advocate-General's opinion.

[19] Case 74/74 *Comptoir National Technique Agricole (CNTA) SA* v. *Commission* [1975] ECR 533, 560 (col. 1) of the Advocate-General's opinion.

[20] Case 210/87 *Remo Padovani and the successors of Otello Mantovani* v. *Amministrazione delle finanze dello Stato* [1988] ECR 6177, para. 32 of Advocate-General Darmon's opinion.

[21] Schwarze, above at n. 2, 867.

dictable.[22] Legal certainty is a basic value of the rule of law and the protection of legitimate expectations promotes certainty and predictability in specific relationships between individuals and the administration.

Another, perhaps more compelling, justification is that "trust in the Community's legal order must be respected".[23] Trust is a basic fact of social life.[24] Under modern conditions of social complexity it is essential for the individual to place trust in government if he is to carry out his activities. A trader may not be able to operate at all without placing a minimum of trust in the Community. Legitimate expectations compels the administration to be trustworthy since an individual may have little choice but to rely upon its conduct. For example, when the applicant in *Mulder* suspended his milk production he was compelled to trust the Community that he would not subsequently be penalised precisely because of this. The protection of such expectations enforces the trust an individual has placed in the administration and prevents the breakdown of a workable relationship between the two. At the same time society as a whole places its trust in the government to judge what the public interest requires. In the event of conflict, protection of the individual's trust should be optimised to the extent that policy goals remain fully attainable.

The principle of legitimate expectations must be distinguished from the related principles of legal certainty and vested rights. Legal certainty requires that "there must be no doubt about the law applicable at a given time in a given area and, consequently, as to the lawful or unlawful nature of certain acts or conduct".[25] This principle has prevented penal statutes having retroactive application[26] and requires that non-penal statutes are generally precluded from taking effect from a point of time before their publication except where the purpose of the measure requires otherwise, and the legitimate expectations of those concerned are respected.[27] Although legal certainty and legitimate expectations are related values which find a common justification in the need for security and predictability, they form distinct principles. Legal certainty is an objective value which places substantive limits on Community acts, whereas legitimate expectations arise as a result of administrative conduct and operate only in the context of a specific relationship between an individual, or a specific class of people,

---

[22] See J. Rawls, *A Theory of Justice* (Clarendon Press, Oxford, 1972), 235–43; J. Raz, "The Rule of Law and Its Virtue", in *The Authority of Law: Essays on Law and Morality* (Oxford, Clarendon Press, 1979), 210.

[23] *Deuka*, above at n. 18, 776 (col. 1) of Advocate-General Trabucchi's opinion.

[24] See N. Luhmann, "Trust: a mechanism for the reduction of social complexity", in *Trust and Power: Two Works by Niklas Luhmann* (Wiley, Chichester, 1979); B.A. Misztal, *Trust in Modern Societies: The Search for the Bases of Social Order* (Polity Press, Cambridge, 1996).

[25] Case C–331/88 R. v. *Minister for Agriculture, Fisheries and Food, ex parte Fedesa* [1990] ECR I–4023, para. 8 of Advocate-General Mischo's opinion.

[26] Case 63/83 R. v. *Kent Kirk* [1984] ECR 2689.

[27] Case 98/78 *Firma A. Racke v. Hauptzollamt Mainz* [1979] ECR 69, para. 20. See F. Lamoureux, "The Retroactivity of Community Acts in the Case Law of the Court of Justice" (1983) 20 *CML Rev.* 269.

and the administration.[28] A vested or acquired right derives from "objective factors inherent in the provisions which in law govern the sector concerned".[29] Such a right is vested or acquired because it is based upon a provision that cannot be withdrawn.[30] A vested right therefore has much more of an absolute character than a legitimate expectation which can be overridden if the public interest so requires.[31]

While the principle of legitimate expectations has a potentially wide scope of application, the European Court has, in practice, imposed a high standard on applicants. A successful claimant must point to some conduct by the administration from which it was reasonable to hold certain expectations. Once induced, expectations may be subject to change. The European Court has consistently maintained that it will protect expectations only where the change was not reasonably foreseeable. Even if the claimant has a reasonable expectation, the administration may argue that it is overridden by the public interest. This requires the court to determine how far an expectation is worthy of protection in the face of a change of policy. Relatively few arguments based on legitimate expectations have succeeded. A claim will prevail only if there is a clear case of unreasonable treatment and the administration grossly misjudged the protection of the individual's expectations. While the principle has "a fairly wide possibility of being invoked . . . [it] . . . is . . . narrowed in its application".[32]

LEGITIMATE EXPECTATIONS IN ENGLISH LAW

It is generally accepted that the principle of legitimate expectations in English law has only developed in recent years.[33] However, it is equally accepted that the phrase "legitimate expectations" had previously been employed in legal and constitutional discourse. For example, in 1881 the Court of Appeal stated that it was a presumption of statutory interpretation that an Act of Parliament was not to be read as interfering with the legal rights or legitimate expectations of any person if the statute would allow that interpretation.[34] At the turn of the

---

[28] Case 161/88 *Binder* v. *Haupzollamt Bad Reichenhall* [1989] ECR 2415, para. 28 of Advocate-General Darmon's opinion.

[29] *CNTA*, above at n. 19, 556 (col. 2) of Advocate-General Trabucchi's opinion.

[30] Joined Cases 7/56 and 3–7/57 *Algera* v. *Common Assembly of the European Coal and Steel Community* [1957–58] ECR 39, 55.

[31] J. Mertens de Wilmars, "The Case-Law of the Court of Justice in Relation to the Review of the Legality of Economic Policy in Mixed-Economy Systems" [1983/1] *Legal Issues of European Integration* 1, 15–16.

[32] D. Edward, "Proportionality and Legitimate Expectations", a talk given at the Judicial Studies Board, 8 January 1993, 89, 98.

[33] See R. Baldwin and D. Horne, "Expectations in a Joyless Landscape" (1986) 49 *MLR* 685; P. Elias, "Legitimate Expectations and Judicial Review", in J. Jowell and D. Oliver (eds), *New Directions in Judicial Review* (Stevens, London, 1988), 37; C.F. Forsyth, "The Provenance and Protection of Legitimate Expectations" (1988) 47 *CLJ* 238; P.P. Craig, "Legitimate Expectations: A Conceptual Analysis" (1992) 108 *LQR* 79.

[34] *In re Barker* (1881) 17 Ch. D 241, 243. See also *Re Lord Penrhyn's Settlement Trusts, Penhryn* v. *Robarts* [1923] 1 Ch. 143, 147; *Re Meux, Gilmour* v. *Gilmour* [1958] Ch. 154, 161.

century the growth of the state had extended to include increased taxation and the acquisition of private property. The idea of legitimate expectations was employed to highlight the perceived unfairness of such activities.[35] The phrase has also been employed by F.A. Hayek in his elaboration of liberal constitutionalism. To protect the individual against the coercive activities of the state, Hayek considered it necessary that the legitimate expectations of individuals be protected by courts that were not concerned with the temporary ends of government but with the long-term aim of upholding the values of a free society.[36] Some rather different meanings have therefore been attributed to legitimate expectations.

The modern origins of the phrase stem from its use by Lord Denning M.R. in *Schmidt* v. *Secretary of State for Home Affairs* [37] which concerned two US citizens who had travelled to the United Kingdom for study purposes. The time limit on their permits had expired and an extension had been refused by the Home Secretary without affording them a hearing. The Court of Appeal held that it was unnecessary to allow the applicants an opportunity to make representations. A hearing would have to take place only where a person had some right or interest or, Lord Denning added, "some legitimate expectation, of which it would not be fair to deprive him without hearing what he has to say".[38] Such a legitimate expectation would arise, Lord Denning continued, if the applicants' permits had been revoked *before* the time limit had expired. In such a case the applicant "ought, I think, to be given an opportunity of making representations; for he would have a legitimate expectation of being allowed to stay for the permitted time".[39] The passing reference to the phrase "legitimate expectation" shines out from the judgment. It had not been mentioned in argument before the court and no authority was cited in support of it. Lord Denning, some twenty years later, commented that his use of the phrase had "came out of my own head and not from any continental or other source".[40] It is testament to Lord Denning's characteristic judicial style that he could introduce a sufficiently unclear phrase in an *obiter* comment which could then be used in subsequent cases to ensure that justice be done.[41]

---

[35] See E. Cannan, *The History of Local Rates in England* (King, London, 2nd ed. 1912), 162–3; G.G. Butler, *The Tory Tradition: Bolingbroke, Burke, Disraeli, Salisbury* [1914](London, Conservative Political Centre, reprinted with a new preface by R.A. Butler, 1957), 12, 45–6.

[36] F.A. Hayek, *The Constitution of Liberty* (Routledge, London, 1960), 217–18.

[37] [1969] 2 Ch. 149.

[38] Ibid., 170F.

[39] Ibid., 171A. See also Widgery L.J. at 173F.

[40] Lord Denning, quoted in Forsyth, above at n. 33, 241. See also *The Denning Interviews—Administrative Law* (Buttwerworths, London, VHS Videocassette, Interviewer: Professor H.W.R. Wade, 1984).

[41] See *Breen* v. *Associated Engineering Union* [1971] 2 QB 175; *McInnes* v. *Onslow Fane* [1978] 3 All ER 211, 218b-g; *O'Reilly* v. *Mackman* [1983] 2 AC 237, 275E-F; *R.* v. *Secretary of State for Transport, ex parte Greater London Council* [1986] 1 QB 556, 587H; *R.* v. *Rochdale Metropolitan Borough Council, ex parte Schemet* (1993) 91 LGR 425, 445–6.

The *Schmidt* case has frequently been cited as the foundation of legitimate expectations in English law.[42] However, the sense in which Lord Denning used it is quite different from its meaning in European law. In *Schmidt* the phrase was intended to give further procedural protection to the applicants if their permits had been revoked before expiry. There was no administrative conduct which could have induced the expectation that they would be given a hearing if the permits were revoked. It would be more accurate to say that the right to be heard in such a situation was based on the deprivation of a "protectable interest", rather than a legitimate expectation.[43] There is a different underlying conceptual basis between the two types of case. Legitimate expectations impose a duty to act fairly, to honour reasonable expectations raised by the conduct of a public authority. Protectable interests may require procedural fairness because the decision threatens the applicant's interests regardless of the previous conduct of the public authority. The protection of legitimate expectations promotes certainty and consistency in administration, which is distinct from the imposition of procedural fairness to a decision which may affect an individual's interests.

Although the *Schmidt* case has been recognised as an instance of legitimate expectations, the use of the phrase in this sense is redundant since the basis of procedural protection is the applicant's interest, so that calling it a legitimate expectation does not make it any stronger.[44] Simon Brown L.J. has considered that this type of case is:[45]

> "no more than a recognition and embodiment of the unsurprising principle that the demands of fairness are likely to be somewhat higher when an authority contemplates depriving someone of an existing benefit or advantage than when the claimant is a bare applicant for a future benefit."

Lord Denning used the phrase to ensure procedural fairness for individuals when the rules of natural justice do not extend to such situations. This involved a sleight of hand: what compels the obligation to have a hearing when the existing law does not so compel? The failure to answer this question explains why so little was said about the content and operation of "legitimate expectation", except by mere reference. It was simply a way of achieving what was considered to be required by justice when more established concepts could not be used. For example, in the *Cinnamond* case[46] Lord Denning held that the expectation of a hearing was not legitimate because of the unmeritorious conduct of the applicants. As Sir Thomas Bingham has noted, the *Schmidt* case "may not amount to parentage" of legitimate expectations.[47]

---

[42] See, e.g., Baldwin and Horne, above at n. 33, 694; B. Hadfield, "Judicial Review and the Concept of Legitimate Expectations" (1988) 39 *NILQ* 103, 104.

[43] See S.A. deSmith, H. Woolf and J. Jowell, *Judicial Review of Administrative Action* (Sweet & Maxwell, London, 5th ed. 1995), 422–4.

[44] P. Cane, *An Introduction to Administrative Law* (Clarendon Press, Oxford, 3rd ed. 1996), 180.

[45] *R. v. Devon County Council, ex parte Baker* [1995] 1 All ER 73, 91a.

[46] *Cinnamond v. British Airports Authority* [1980] 2 All ER 368.

[47] Sir Thomas Bingham, "'There is a World Elsewhere': The Changing Perspectives of English

Another decision cited in support of the principle is the *Liverpool Taxis* case.[48] A local authority had proposed to increase the number of taxis and had made an undertaking to the effect that the existing taxicab owners would be consulted before any decision was made. However, the authority subsequently confirmed a resolution to increase the number of taxis without allowing any prior consultation. The Court of Appeal found this to be unlawful. Lord Denning stated that the authority was not at liberty to disregard its undertaking and should have departed from it only after hearing what the other party had to say, and then only if the overriding public interest required it. However, the basis upon which the authority was bound by its undertaking was obscure. Neither the duty to act fairly nor legitimate expectation were mentioned. As Gabriele Ganz noted, the undertaking "sprang autochthonally from the case itself. It was in later cases that the link was made between legitimate expectation and the *Liverpool Corporation Case*".[49]

The question concerning the origins of legitimate expectations in English law would therefore appear to be unclear. However, it is submitted that the development of the principle from the early 1980s onwards has been influenced in part by the existence of the same principle as interpreted in European law. In 1977 Lord Diplock acknowledged the need to assimilate the European principle into English law.[50] While Lord Denning's use of the phrase does not appear to have been influenced by the European principle, other judges, such as Lord Diplock, have used that phrase to develop a similar concept to that which exists in European law. John Usher has explained that when the European Court decided to apply the *vertrauensschutz* principle it was translated into French, being the working language of the court, as *"protection de la confiance légitime"*.[51] While this was translated into English originally as "legitimate confidence", it was later changed to "legitimate expectation" because of the technical meaning of confidence in English law. It may have been the case that the label "legitimate expectation" was then used by commentators to describe the concept as applied by the European court, even though they had different meanings.[52] Regardless of the labels used, it is clear that the principle of legitimate expectations in English law has developed as a response to the principle in European law. Equally important is the fact that some judges have explicitly drawn upon the European jurisprudence in order to develop English law. For instance, Sedley J., as he then was, has remarked that while Britain is "a relative

---

Law" (1992) 41 *ICLQ* 513, 523, n. 34. According to Sir John Laws, *Schmidt* cannot "be said to have established the doctrine in England": "English and Community Law: Uniformity of Principle", *The European Advocate* (Autumn, 1994), 2.

[48] R. v. *Liverpool Corporation, ex parte Liverpool Taxi Fleet Operators' Association* [1972] 2 QB 299.

[49] G. Ganz, "Legitimate Expectation: A Confusion of Concepts", in C. Harlow (ed.), *Public Law and Politics* (Sweet & Maxwell, London, 1986), 145, 150.

[50] *Hansard*, H.L. Deb, Vol. 379, cols 993–4, 3 February 1977.

[51] J.A. Usher, *General Principles of EC Law* (Longman, London, 1998), 54.

[52] This is suggested by Forsyth, above at n. 33, 242, n. 22.

newcomer to the doctrine . . . [t]his . . . may be an advantage, at least to the extent that our case law on the topic has not had a chance to ossify and because it *enables us to learn from our neighbours*".[53]

The confusion caused by Lord Denning's usage of the phrase has been compounded subsequently by other judges attempting to find a suitable conceptualisation of the principle. When Lord Diplock first referred to legitimate expectations he emphasised that it belonged to public law and gave the applicant a sufficient interest to challenge the legality of the decision.[54] However, other judges have not always approached the matter in the same way. Lord Templeman has stated that unfairness by a public authority would amount to an abuse of power if it were equivalent to a breach of contract or a breach of representation,[55] while Stuart Smith L.J. has remarked that the principle of legitimate expectations has many similarities with the private law principle of estoppel.[56] The conceptual uncertainty over whether the principle forms part of a distinct administrative law or whether it is simply the consequences of private law principles betrays the lack of a coherent basis for public law. Further uncertainty has been evidenced by judicial comments suggesting that the principle has a limited role in giving the individual a sufficient interest to challenge a decision.[57] As Parker L.J. noted, this "is a long way from being entitled to succeed in such a challenge".[58] To the extent that Lord Denning's use of the phrase is still classified as a category of legitimate expectation proper[59] and that the principle is sometimes viewed as deriving from estoppel, there remains a lack of conceptual clarity concerning its precise application. Lord Fraser described the principle as "somewhat lacking in precision".[60] While it has commonly been stated that the principle is rooted in fairness, it is unclear whether judges have meant fairness in the sense of the rules of natural justice or fairness in the sense of requiring a public authority to act consistently with the expectations it has induced. This ambiguity has allowed some to argue that it is a purely procedural principle and cannot confer any substantive benefit.[61] Simon Brown L.J. acknowledged that "many semantic confusions . . . have bedevilled this area of

---

[53] R. v. *Ministry of Agriculture, Fisheries and Food, ex parte Hamble (Offshore) Fisheries Ltd.* [1995] 2 All ER 714, 725g (emphasis added).

[54] *O'Reilly* v. *Mackman*, above at n. 41, 275E; *Council of Civil Service Unions* v. *Minister for the Civil Service* [1985] AC 374, 408H (the *GCHQ* case).

[55] *In re Preston* [1985] AC 835, 866H–7A.

[56] R. v. *Jockey Club, ex parte RAM Racecourses Ltd.* [1993] 2 All ER 225, 236h–j. See also *Oloniluyi* v. *Home Secretary* [1990] Imm. AR 135, 146. In R. v. *Independent Television Commission, ex parte TSW Broadcasting Ltd.* (1992) unreported, 5 February, CA, Lord Donaldson M.R. stated that "[t]he test in public law is fairness, not an adaptation of the law of contract or estoppel".

[57] *O'Reilly* v. *Mackman*, above at n. 41, 275E; *Findlay* v. *Secretary of State for the Home Department* [1985] AC 318, 338D.

[58] R. v. *Secretary of State for the Home Department, ex parte Khan* [1985] 1 All ER 40, 46h.

[59] See, e.g., C.F. Forsyth, "*Wednesbury* Protection of Substantive Legitimate Expectations" [1997] PL 375, 377.

[60] *Attorney-General of Hong Kong* v. *Ng Yuen Shiu* [1983] 2 AC 629, 636D.

[61] See below at pp. 60–1.

our law".[62] To this we may add that conceptual confusion has also characterised the use of legitimate expectations by the English courts.

While the principle of legitimate expectations developed in European law as the integration of a progressive doctrine from a national legal order, English courts have largely refused to recognise its Continental origins. Instead, they have preferred to keep its meaning vague and obscure. The reasons for this are clear. English judges feel that they cannot allow themselves to be seen to be openly making new law for fear of offending the democratic arm of government. They must pretend merely to be declaring the law as it has always been. The notion that the law can play a socially useful role in facilitating administrative objectives and rationalising the impact of decisions for individuals is alien to the common law tradition. As the courts have developed judicial review to compensate for the inadequacies of Parliamentary accountability, the focus has been on individual fairness rather than purposive rationality. The principle of legitimate expectations has been approached by English judges from this perspective. Judges have seen the utility of the principle for promoting fairness. However, they have not acknowledged legitimate expectations as a public law principle requiring the court to promote policy objectives constructively. This has caused uncertainty and confusion over the role of the principle. This difference of approach is reflected in the legal apparatus used by the administration. In the European Community the institutions adopt rules or regulations for ends specified under the Treaties. Principles which condition the achievement of such ends are seen as a necessary feature of legitimate administration, whereas in English law public authorities typically have wide discretionary powers conferred upon them by statute, for which no ends are specified and the imposition of any principles is seen as an illegitimate interference with such power. As English courts tend to refuse to undertake a more constructive role in administration they retreat into vague assessments of unreasonableness.

Furthermore, there is a deeply held belief, exemplified in Dicey's work, that the common law has little to learn from Continental systems of administrative law. Few judges today would view French administrative law as a protector of administrative arbitrariness, and there are signs of an increased willingness on the part of some judges to refer to European doctrines. However, the dominant tradition rooted in the common law of England still retains a strong hold over judicial minds. It is implicitly accepted that English law should pay little regard to how things are done elsewhere, and judges occasionally articulate their discomfort with the European influence. For example, the judgment of Sedley J. in the *Hamble* case was justifiably commended for its attention to European law and scholarship, and the willingness to develop legitimate expectations by assimilating English and European law. It is therefore unfortunate, although hardly surprising, that higher judges later rejected this "heretical" judgment without addressing such concerns or even seeking a proper understanding of what was

---

[62] *Baker*, above at n. 45, 89h.

being discussed.[63] The underlying assumption here is that Continental law, not being founded upon the practical experience of the common law, is somehow inferior. Other judges consider that the principle of legitimate expectations reflects established common law principles, such as estoppel. As the common law has not traditionally made any distinction between public and private law, this approach has fitted legitimate expectations within the universal conception of legality. This has merely contributed to the uncertainty and confusion over the role and meaning of the principle. The effective integration of the principle has been hampered by conceptual uncertainty and an unwillingness to take advantage of European jurisprudence in preference for customary common law doctrines.

The application of legitimate expectations can have significant practical implications. Since the protection of legitimate expectations may require a reorganisation of policy implementation, it is essential that the courts are informed of the needs of public administration and aware of the consequences of their decisions.[64] From the administrator's perspective, judicial uncertainty over the scope of the principle can be particularly unhelpful.[65] For example, the controversy over whether the principle is merely procedural or whether it also protects substantive benefits can create administrative uncertainty over precisely what requirements public authorities will have imposed on them. While the courts have stated that a clear and unambiguous representation is required for an expectation to be raised,[66] their own elaboration of the principle has at times been far removed from such a standard, thereby diminishing legal certainty for both the administration and individuals.

It has been suggested that the principle should be able to contribute to the structuring of discretionary power by informing the administration of the values of honesty, open-mindedness and consistency.[67] Perhaps the biggest impediment to this structuring of discretion is the relative lack of specialist judicial knowledge of governmental processes, combined with the unwillingness to review findings of fact made by the administration. English courts have traditionally viewed their role as separate from administration, and having a practical experience in common law is considered more important than knowledge of public administration. The risk is that if judicial conceptions of "fairness" are not informed by an understanding of the administration, they may turn out to be little more than ritualistic incantations of the justice of common law. This

---

[63] *Hamble*, above at n. 53; *R. v. Secretary of State for the Home Department, ex parte Hargreaves* [1997] 1 All ER 397. See below at p. 71.

[64] See J.W.F. Allison, "The Procedural Reason for Judicial Restraint" [1994] *PL* 452.

[65] S. James, "The Political and Administrative Consequences of Judicial Review" (1996) 74 *Public Administration* 613, 624.

[66] *R. v. Inland Revenue Commissioners, ex parte MFK Underwriting Agents Ltd.* [1990] 1 WLR 1545, 1569G.

[67] D. Feldman, "Judicial Review: A Way of Controlling Government?" (1988) 66 *Public Administration* 21, 27.

obfuscates the difficulties of ensuring that complex public policy programmes can be carried out effectively and equitably.

Recent cases have suggested that the application of the principle could be having an educative effect on the administration. For example, the adoption of transitional provisions suggests that the administration acknowledges the need to take special account of individuals caught between changes of policy.[68] However, in other cases the administration has responded by attempting to ensure that no further expectations can be created.[69] In the *Khan* decision,[70] the Court of Appeal upheld an expectation in light of a change of criteria for the adoption of children from overseas. Following this decision, the Home Office responded by "reducing the specificity and precision" of the guidance.[71] If courts are to protect such expectations they must also be prepared to require greater certainty and precision in administrative guidelines, otherwise any positive benefit derived from the principle could be undermined.

INDUCEMENT OF EXPECTATIONS

For an individual to invoke the principle, an expectation must have been induced by some conduct of the administration. The European Court has recognised that the principle extends to any individual who is in a situation in which it appears that the administration's conduct has led him to entertain certain expectations.[72] The notion of trust implies placing reliance on incomplete and unreliable information, which is not enough, in itself, to guarantee success. An individual overdraws what information is available in order to anticipate the future conduct of the administration. The principle protects only those expectations which have arisen through administrative conduct, and not those which have arisen as a result of an individual's subjective hopes. It is concerned with upholding trust in the administration rather than protecting expectations which the individual has decided to entertain at his own risk.

Both the European Court and the English courts have stated that the principle must not become a free-standing claim by an individual, but must be based upon some conduct by the administration. For example, in the *Mulder* case the applicant's expectations had been created by entering into the non-marketing undertaking. This is to be contrasted with the subsequent case of *Kuhn*.[73] Here the applicant had not made an undertaking but had leased his farm over the

---

[68] Transitional provisions were adopted in *Hamble*, above at n. 53, 720j, and *Hargreaves*, above at n. 63, 400g.
[69] See M. Kerry, "Administrative Law and Judicial Review—The Practical Effects of Developments Over the Last 25 Years in Administration in Central Government" (1986) 64 *Public Administration* 163, 170.
[70] *Khan*, above at n. 58.
[71] A.R. Mowbray, "Administrative Guidance and Judicial Review" [1985] *PL* 558, 563.
[72] Case 289/81 *Mavrides* v. *European Parliament* [1983] ECR 1731, para. 21.
[73] Case C–177/90 *Kuhn* v. *Landwirtschaftskammer Weser-Ems* [1992] ECR I–35.

period in which the reference quantity was to be calculated. During that period the lessees had mismanaged the farm and deliberately reduced milk production. The applicant could not therefore show a representative level of milk deliveries for the reference year. The European Court rejected the claim that there was a breach of legitimate expectations because there was no conduct on behalf of the Community which had induced the applicant to lease his farm. He had done so at his own risk.

Legitimate expectations can also arise as a result of administrative practices. In a 1987 case the European Court invalidated a Commission decision to impose a fine on a steel producer for exceeding a production quota because of the existence of a continuing practice on behalf of the Commission to tolerate the disposal of stock in addition to the delivery quota.[74] The producer had relied on the practice, which had operated for two-years and which had given rise consequently to a legitimate expectation.

The European Court has also been prepared to allow inactivity by the administration to induce a legitimate expectation. If the administration delays a decision for a sufficiently long period of time this may create an expectation of a favourable result. For example, in one case the Commission took twenty-six months to decide whether a subsidy granted by a Member State was compatible with Community rules.[75] The European Court held that this delay had given rise to reasonable grounds for believing that the state aid was lawful. However, if the applicant is in part responsible for the delay, this will count against the reasonableness of the expectation.[76]

The position in English law is analogous. It is recognised that while legitimate expectation is concerned with fairness towards the individual, it is also concerned with legal certainty for pubic authorities. Therefore, the courts require administrative conduct to induce an expectation, rather than merely imply promises into relationships.[77] Lord Fraser stated that:[78]

"Legitimate, or reasonable, expectation may arise from an express promise given on behalf of a public authority or from the existence of a regular practice which the claimant can reasonably expect to continue."

An example of express statement is the *Ng Yuen Shiu* case.[79] Illegal Chinese immigrants in Hong Kong had been told by the authorities that they would each be interviewed concerning their specific situation and, although there was no guarantee that they would remain, each case would be treated on its merits.

---

[74] Case 344/85 *Ferriere San Carlo* v. *Commission* [1987] ECR 4435. See also Case 129/87 *Decker* v. *Caisse de pension des employés privés* [1988] ECR 6121.

[75] Case 223/85 *Rijn-Schelde-Verolme (RSV) Machinefabrieken en Scheepswerven NV* v. *Commission* [1987] ECR 4617. See also Case 127/80 *Grogan* v. *Commission* [1982] ECR 869.

[76] Case C–303/88 *Italy* v. *Commission* [1991] ECR I–1433.

[77] *R.* v. *Secretary of State for Education, ex parte London Borough of Southwark* [1995] 1 ELR 308, 320.

[78] *GCHQ*, above at n. 54, 401B.

[79] *Ng Yuen Shiu*, above at n. 60.

Despite this assurance the applicant was refused a hearing. Lord Fraser, speaking for the Privy Council, assumed that the applicant's position as an illegal immigrant would not, in itself, afford him a right to be heard. However, a legitimate expectation to a hearing existed because of the express statement made by the authorities. If an authority has promised to follow a certain procedure it is in the interests of good administration for it to act fairly and implement its promise. In the *GCHQ* case[80] the House of Lords accepted that there was an expectation for the civil service unions to be consulted over any change in working conditions of the staff at Government Communications Head Quarters because of the consistent practice of consultation. Legitimate expectations have also arisen through the setting out of policies.[81]

CHANGE OF EXPECTATIONS

Only reasonable expectations will be afforded protection by the law. An individual must hold an expectation which it was reasonable to have in light of all the circumstances. If the possibility of change was reasonably foreseeable then it will not be reasonable to maintain the same expectations as before. As the principle has largely been applied in matters of economic administration in Community law where changes in the situation are frequent, the need to foresee changes in expectations has been a critical feature in the European Court's case law. The principle of legitimate expectations has been applied in relation to the operation of monetary compensatory amounts which were introduced in the 1970s to compensate for changes in exchange rates. As rates can fluctuate quickly the Community also needed to respond quickly. The European Court placed high requirements on traders seeking to establish an expectation worthy of protection. The reasonable and prudent trader is expected to be aware of the inherent uncertainties of a situation, and to be well-informed about the possibilities of any change. For example, if a proposal is made by the Commission to change the applicable compensatory amounts then this should alert the experienced trader.[82] To claim a legitimate expectation successfully any interference must have occurred without warning, with immediate effect and without any transitional measures which a prudent trader could have used to avoid losses. As Lord Mackenzie Stuart commented:[83]

> "[T]he Court is less susceptible . . . to the blandishments of the large and experienced undertaking well able to see in which direction the economic wind is blowing and able to make for a safe anchorage before the storm cloud breaks."

[80] *GCHQ*, above at n. 54. See also R. v. *British Coal Corporation, ex parte Vardy* [1993] ICR 720.

[81] *Khan*, above at n. 58; R. v. *Secretary of State for the Home Department, ex parte Ruddock* [1987] 1 WLR 1482.

[82] Joined Cases 95 to 98/74, 15 and 100/75, *Union Nationale des Coopératives Agricoles de Céréales* v. *Commission and Council* [1975] ECR 1615, para. 45.

[83] Lord Mackenzie Stuart, *The European Communities and the Rule of Law* (Stevens, London, 1977), 96.

English courts have not had to apply the principle in such conditions, and therefore have not stressed the possibility of change in expectations to the same degree as the European Court. However, there is a similarity in the underlying principle that the individual must be aware that expectations are subject to change. In *Hughes* v. *Department of Health and Social Security*[84] Lord Diplock recognised that expectations created by an administrative circular will be destroyed and replaced by new expectations when a new circular announces a change in policy.

LEGALITY AND EXPECTATIONS

The relationship between the principles of legitimate expectations and legality raises fundamental issues of how to reconcile conflicting interests. If the conduct of the public authority which induced an expectation is itself outside the legal power of the authority, can a legitimate expectation exist? The problem requires some reconciliation of the trust an individual has placed in such expectations and the need for the administration to keep within its legal powers. Before comparing the position in European and English law, the approach of other Member States will be examined.

The position in German administrative law is that if the administration has induced expectations beyond the limits of its power, the administrative court will resolve the conflict by balancing the interests in legality with those of legal certainty. In a case decided in 1956 a widow moved from East to West Germany after being told that she would be entitled to welfare benefits, which she received for a period. However, the administration subsequently decided that the payments had not been lawful. The payments ceased and the widow was required to repay what she had received. The Berlin Administrative Court held that the conflict between legality and legal certainty needed to be reconciled by an *ad hoc* balancing test.[85] In this case the court decided to uphold the widow's expectations that the payments had been made lawfully. Following this decision the drafting of the German Administrative Procedure Act 1976 included a provision to cover this type of situation. Section 48(2) states:[86]

> "An unlawful administrative decision granting a pecuniary benefit may not be revoked insofar as the beneficiary has relied upon the decision and his expectation, weighed against the public interest in revoking the decision, merits protection."

Under Dutch administrative law legitimate expectations contrary to the strict application of the law may be protected if the individual concerned acted

---

[84] [1985] AC 776, 788B–C.

[85] Decision of the Berlin *Oberverwaltungsgericht* (1957) 72 *Deustches Verwaltungsblatt* 503; affirmed by the Federal Administrative Court (*Bundesverwaltungsgericht*) (1959) 9 BwerGE 251.

[86] Translation taken from Joined Cases 205 to 215/82 *Deutsche Milchkontor GmbH* v. *Germany* [1983] ECR 2633, para. 28. See also M.P. Singh, *German Administrative Law in Common Law Perspective* (Springer-Verlag, Berlin, 1985), 46.

in reliance on the expectation and the interests of third parties are not affected.[87] The law of at least two of the Member States therefore allows for the possibility of protecting expectations which have arisen outside the strict application of the law.

By contrast, the European Court has refused to admit the possibility of protecting expectations which have arisen as a consequence of unlawful administrative activity. In the *Maizena* case[88] an applicant challenged the decision of a German customs office demanding repayment of a production refund. The method for calculating the production refund was contrary to the applicable Community rules and the applicant claimed a legitimate expectation that this practice would not be departed from by the German authorities. The European Court rejected the argument, stating:[89]

"A practice of a Member State which does not conform to Community rules may never give rise to legal situations protected by Community law and this is even so where the Commission has failed to take the necessary action to ensure that the State in question correctly applies the Community rules."

More recently, in its *Air France* decision,[90] the Court of First Instance ruled that from the hierarchy of legal rules laid down in the Treaties it follows that "a Community institution cannot be forced, by virtue of the principle of legitimate expectations, to apply Community rules *contra legem*".

English law has adopted a similar stance. Primacy must always be given to the *ultra vires* rule because otherwise public authorities would be able to extend their powers at will.[91] Lord Denning's attempts to prevent a public authority resiling from an *ultra vires* representation through the principle of estoppel[92] have effectively been limited by the Court of Appeal.[93] More recently, Sedley J. endorsed the view that the application of legitimate expectation was restricted by the jurisdiction of the public authority. The dual effect of applying the principle in this "prohibited area" would be to extend the statutory power of the public authority and destroy the *ultra vires* rule by permitting authorities to

---

[87] R. Widdershoven and R. de Lange, "Dutch Report", in J. Schwarze (ed.), *Administrative Law Under European Influence: On the convergence of the administrative laws of EU Member States* (Sweet & Maxwell, London, 1996), 529, 569–70. See also C.J. Bax, "Judicial Control of the Administration in the Netherlands" (1992) 4 *European Review of Public Law* 71, 76–7.

[88] Case 5/82 *Hauptzollamt Krefeld* v. *Maizena GmbH* [1982] ECR 4601. See also Case 1252/79 *SpA Acciaierie e Ferriere Lucchini* v. *Commission* [1980] ECR 3753; Case 316/86 *Hauptzollamt Hamburg-Jonas* v. *Krücken* [1988] ECR 2213.

[89] Ibid., para. 22.

[90] Case T–2/93 *Societe Anonyme a Participation Ouvriere Compagnie Nationale Air France* v. *Commission* [1994] ECR II–323, para. 102.

[91] *Ministry of Agriculture and Fisheries* v. *Hunkin* (1948) unreported, but cited in *Ministry of Agriculture and Fisheries* v. *Matthews* [1950] 1 KB 148, 153–4.

[92] *Robertson* v. *Minister of Pensions* [1949] 1 KB 227; *Falmouth Boat Construction Co.* v. *Howell* [1950] 1 KB 16; *Wells* v. *Minister of Housing and Local Government* [1967] 1 WLR 1000; *Lever Finance Ltd.* v. *Westminster Borough Council* [1971] 1 QB 222.

[93] *Western Fish Products* v. *Penwith District Council* [1981] 2 All ER 204. See also *Maritime Electric Co.* v. *General Dairies Ltd.* [1937] AC 610.

extend their own powers at will.[94] The restriction of the principle in this way has been questioned in both European and English law.[95]

A PROCEDURAL OR SUBSTANTIVE PRINCIPLE?

Is legitimate expectations a purely procedural principle or can it also be used to protect expectations of a substantive nature? This has been a contentious issue in English law.[96] Since many of the early cases concerned expectations that a certain procedure would be used, it was thought that the doctrine was limited and could not be extended to substantive benefits. However, there has been a difference of opinion on this issue. For instance, Taylor J. considered that "while most of the cases are concerned . . . with a right to be heard, I do not think that the doctrine can be so confined".[97] In the opinion of Sir Louis Blom-Cooper Q.C., the principle is of an exclusively procedural nature: "[i]t cannot be extended to encompass any substantive right".[98] This issue has been one of the main difficulties of the principle for English courts. In contrast, the European Court has never drawn a distinction between procedural and substantive expectations. Since the Community provides for extensive consultation before the adoption of a measure, the use of legitimate expectations in procedural matters is "not really a problem in Community law".[99] Furthermore, the European Court simply does not adopt the dualistic classification between procedure and substance to which the English courts have clung. In light of the importance of substantive review in German administrative law[100] the European Court would have been viewed as providing only a limited and ineffective form of judicial protection if it had drawn a similar distinction between procedural and substantive expectations.

Recent judicial discussion of the scope of legitimate expectations in English law began with a judgment of Laws J. in a case concerning the regulation of aircraft noise at night.[101] The Secretary of State had a statutory power to control aircraft movements. In 1988 measures were introduced to limit aircraft movements at night at the London airports. These measures were due to expire in

---

[94] *Hamble*, above at n. 53, 731g–h. See also R. Singh, "Making Legitimate Use of Legitimate Expectation" (1994) 144 *NLJ* 1215.

[95] See the opinion of Advocate-General Darmon in Case 210/87 *Padovani*, above at n. 20, para. 32 and *Binder*, above at n. 28, para. 9; P.P. Craig, *Administrative Law* (Sweet & Maxwell, London, 4th ed. 1999), 635–50.

[96] See P.P. Craig, "Substantive Legitimate Expectations in Domestic and Community Law" (1996) 55 *CLJ* 289.

[97] *Ruddock*, above at n. 81, 1497A. See also *Chundawadra* v. *Immigration Appeal Tribunal* [1988] Imm. AR 161, 172, 175.

[98] *R.* v. *Council of the Borough of Poole, ex parte Cooper* (1995) 27 HLR 605, 614.

[99] *Edward*, above at n. 32, 96.

[100] See Nolte, above at n. 3.

[101] *R.* v. *Secretary of State for Transport, ex parte Richmond upon Thames London Borough Council* [1994] 1 All ER 577.

1993 and replaced by a quota system in which types of aircraft would be assigned a quota number. Under the quota system airlines would be able to decide which types of aircraft could be used in order to fill up their quota. A press notice stated that the new quota policy was designed to keep the overall noise levels below those of 1988. On the basis of this undertaking the applicant local authorities claimed a legitimate expectation that the policy of noise levels would not be taken beyond the 1988 levels under any circumstances. In order to claim such an expectation, it was argued that the principle extended to substantive benefits. This argument was rejected. In the opinion of Laws J., legitimate expectations could require a public authority not to change its existing policy without giving those affected a right to be heard. However, it could not be extended so as to afford a substantive expectation that a policy would not be changed even though those affected had been consulted. Three reasons were advanced in support of this. First, there was no previous authority on which to justify the protection of a substantive expectation. Secondly, if the principle did extend to substantive expectations it would impose an unacceptable fetter on the power of a public authority to change its policy when it considered this necessary for the fulfilment of its public responsibilities. Thirdly, Laws J. stated that if substantive expectations were to be protected then the court would have to decide whether the public interest required the individual's expectation to be overridden. This would entail the court judging the merits of the public interest and the proposed policy change, which would be an illegitimate interference with the merits of public decisions. Alternatively, Laws J. reasoned that if this were incorrect, then all the court could do was decide whether the proposed policy change was unreasonable in the *Wednesbury* sense.[102]

This reasoning is open to question. Laws J. appeared to assume that the protection of substantive legitimate expectations could preclude a public authority from changing its general policy. However, there is nothing in the jurisprudence of the European Court to support this view. That Court has consistently stated that individuals cannot legitimately expect that an existing situation, which is capable of being altered by the Community institutions in the exercise of their discretionary power, will be maintained.[103] Legitimate expectation cannot be used to prevent the administration from adopting new policies. However, it does require administrators to give special attention to individuals who hold certain expectations when a policy change is undertaken. The argument was presented in a way which suggested that the principle could be used to prevent a public authority from changing its policy, and on this basis, the possibility of substantive expectations was rejected. Laws J. stated that there was no case "in which it has been held that there exists an enforceable expectation that a policy

---

[102] *Associated Provincial Pictures Houses Ltd.* v. *Wednesbury Corporation* [1948] 1 KB 223.
[103] See Case 245/81 *Edeka Zentrale AG* v. *Germany* [1982] ECR 2745; Joined Cases 424 and 425/85 *Coöperatieve Melkproducentenbedrijven Noord-Nederland BA ("Frico")* v. *Voedselvoorzienings In- en Verkoopbureau* [1987] ECR 2755; Case C–305/88 *Société française des Biscuits Delacre* v. *Commission* [1990] ECR I–395.

will not be changed *even though* those affected have been consulted about any policy change".[104] This is certainly correct. In *Khan*[105] the Court of Appeal did not prevent the Home Secretary from changing the policy criteria concerning overseas adoption, but it did require the applicant to be excepted from the application of the new policy. Legitimate expectations safeguarded the special position of the applicant within the change of policy. A policy change *vis-à-vis* the applicant could be achieved only after a hearing had been afforded to him and then only if the overriding public interest required it.

The argument that protecting substantive expectations would fetter the power of public authorities to change their policy is also untenable. If the principle did operate to emasculate policy or fetter discretionary power it would represent an illegitimate brake on the exercise of public power. However, the principle does not prevent changes of general policy, but instead relates to circumstances where an individual holds certain expectations within such changes of policy. Two policies may be perfectly lawful but can create unfairness for the individual if the public authority changes its policy after raising an expectation in the individual's mind that it would act in a certain way. The public authority must respect the trust an individual has placed in its conduct. Even then it can be argued that public interest requires the individual to be treated on the terms of the new policy. None of this fetters the policy-making power because it is not legitimate to expect public policies to stand still.

The third reason advanced by Laws J. was that if the court had to decide whether there was an overriding public interest which required the disappointment of an expectation then the court would be judging the merits of the public interest and the proposed policy change. The sleight of hand here is to assimilate the identification of the public interest with the task of deciding which means should be used to achieve those objectives. It confuses ends with means. The court cannot substitute its view of the policy objectives for that of the public authority, but it can examine whether the frustration of the individual's expectation is necessary for the achievement of those objectives. If the administration could use alternative means which were equally capable of achieving the same objective, but which also accommodated the individual's expectations, the court should confirm those expectations as legitimate. This does not require the court to substitute its view of the public interest for that of the administration, but to insist that, so far as possible, individuals are treated with sensitivity.

Despite an evident disapproval of substantive expectations, Laws J. did recognise that the doctrine was rooted in the ideal of fairness. What is unclear is the sense in which "fairness" was employed. Did it mean procedural fairness for protectable interests, or did it require a public body to act consistently in light

---

[104] *Richmond*, above at n. 101, 598a.
[105] *Khan*, above at n. 58.

of raised expectations?[106] This ambiguity reflects continuing uncertainty over the doctrine. In an attempt to clarify the issue Sedley J. subsequently used the notion of the duty to act fairly in order to justify substantive expectations:[107]

"[T]he real question is one of fairness in public administration. It is difficult to see why it is any less unfair to frustrate a legitimate expectation that something will or will not be done by the decision-maker than it is to frustrate a legitimate expectation that the applicant will be listened to before the decision-maker decides whether to take a particular step."

The need to protect legitimate expectations of a substantive benefit was, for Sedley J., as much in the interests of fairness as the need to uphold expectations of a certain procedure. This reasoning is coherent. If a legitimate expectation imposes a duty to act fairly, in the sense of acting consistently with regard to the expectation it induced, then there is no reason why this should be limited solely to procedural expectations. Any distinction between procedural and substantive expectations is artificial. While the reasoning of Sedley J. has done much to clarify the debate, the matter is not free from doubt. Lord Steyn has noted, *obiter*, that the precise scope of the principle is "a controversial question".[108]

The issue of whether legitimate expectations is a procedural principle or can extend to substantive benefits has troubled the English courts. By comparison, the European Court accepted without hesitation that the principle encompassed the protection of expectations of a substantive nature. Why has there been such a divergent approach? The answer, it is submitted, lies in the underlying approach to law and administration. The European Court has been able to use law as a means of advancing the policy objectives of the Community and rationalising their impact on individuals. If our conception of law is constituted on the purpose the administration seeks to achieve, it is unnecessary to draw any distinction between procedure and substance. The administrative court is concerned with optimising the individual's expectation to the extent that attainment of the public purpose remains factually possible. There is little danger of substantive review collapsing into appeal on the merits because the court is concerned to ensure that the administration's goal is achieved. Questions about policy application are not to be avoided. On the contrary, it is precisely the role of an administrative jurisdiction to ensure the fair implementation of policy. In comparison the review exercised by English courts has traditionally focused solely on the decision-making process.[109] The courts have adopted a deferential approach to substantive matters for fear of becoming embroiled in policy issues.

---

[106] Elsewhere, Sir John Laws has stated that "[t]he doctrine of legitimate expectations has, as its parent, the old notion of natural justice": "Is the High Court the Guardian of Fundamental Constitutional Rights?" [1993] *PL* 59, 68.

[107] *Hamble*, above at n. 53, 724b–c. Sedley J. at 724g stated that "[s]ince some of the leading cases in the Court of Justice concern legitimate expectations of substantive benefits or protections in the face of policy shifts, they furnish further support for the view that I have expressed . . . on this topic".

[108] *Pierson* v. *Secretary of State for the Home Department* [1997] 3 All ER 577, 606f.

[109] See, e.g., *Chief Constable of North Wales* v. *Evans* [1982] 3 All ER 141, 155c.

The consequence of this is that English courts have felt uncomfortable with regard to the protection of substantive expectations. Lacking the confidence to require the administration to take account of such expectations, the courts have sought to avoid the issue by drawing the distinction between procedure and substance. However, this dualistic way of thinking is highly artificial. It is difficult to draw such distinctions with any clarity. The unwillingness to use law to promote policy goals has meant that the courts have restricted protection of the individual's trust in government. Since such protection can enhance the acceptability of administrative decision-making, it is arguable that the courts have failed to promote a more co-operative relationship between the individual and the State. In contrast, the European Court has not drawn any line between the protection of procedural and substantive expectations because it adopts a goal-oriented review. In light of this, the *Hamble* judgment is a welcome reminder to English judges not to get caught up in artificial distinctions.[110]

There is also a degree of uncertainty in English law over the application of legitimate expectations with regard to secondary legislation. Neill L.J. has expressed doubts over whether, save in exceptional cases, the principle could be invoked to invalidate primary or secondary legislation.[111] While it would not be expected that English courts would enforce legitimate expectations against an Act of Parliament, the restriction with regard to secondary legislation seems unjustifiable. Policies are implemented by such law-making, and this restriction constitutes an anomalous restriction on the applicability of the principle.[112] In contrast, the European Court has invalidated Council regulations to protect expectations.[113] Again, English courts appear to prefer artificial distinctions over contributing towards successful governance.

BALANCING THE INTERESTS: THE LEGITIMACY OF AN EXPECTATION

Where an expectation has been held to be reasonable it is necessary to determine whether it has a legitimacy which makes it worthy of protection. The administrative court must examine whether the expectation is sustainable in light of a policy change by the administration. For an individual to have placed confidence in his expectations is to have anticipated his future relationship with the administration. The protection of such expectations therefore concerns the temporal dimension of how far they can be sustained in light of the changing

---

[110] A parallel development can be traced in another judgment by Sedley J. in *R. v. Secretary of State for the Environment, ex parte Kirkwood Valley Campaign Ltd.* [1996] 3 All ER 304.

[111] *R. v. Secretary of State for the Environment, ex parte National and Local Government Officers' Association* [1993] 5 Admin. LR 785, 804E.

[112] For instance, the courts have declared secondary legislation approved by Parliament to be invalid in *R. v. HM Treasury, ex parte Smedley* [1985] QB 657 (improper purpose); *R. v. Secretary of State for the Home Department, ex parte Leech* [1994] QB 198 (legal professional privilege).

[113] See, e.g., *Mulder*, above at n. 9. The *Bundesverfassungericht* has ruled that *vertrauensschutz* is a constitutional principle: see Nolte, above at n. 3, 203.

circumstances and needs of public administration. Achievement of the public interest cannot be dependent upon whether or not it interferes with an individual's expectation. At the same time, the individual deserves distinct consideration because of the confidence he has placed in his expectations. The individual has placed personal investment on the basis of his expectations which now needs to be accommodated as far as possible within the implementation of new policy goals.

How should the administrative court resolve this conflict? The approach of the European Court is to undertake a balancing exercise of the competing interests to determine whether the expectation has legitimacy. It is for the administration to determine the requirements of the public interest and how to achieve them. If the public interest requires a policy change, the administration will have to decide whether the means to be used necessitate the disappointment of any expectations. The initial balance is therefore a task for the administration. However, if an individual claims that his expectations have been unjustifiably or unnecessarily disappointed, the court will review whether there was a proportionate relationship between the public objective sought and the measure adopted. It is clear that if the public interest would be undermined by extending protection to the expectation then it must be overridden. As Advocate-General Trabucchi has commented, "[w]hen the public interest so requires there can be no doubt that the interests of individuals, even if they form a group of some size, must take second place".[114] The purpose of the review exercised by the European Court is not to substitute its view of the desired public interest for that of the administrator, but to determine whether the disappointment of an expectation was indispensable for the attainment of that objective. In this section the different judicial approaches to this issue will be compared. First, the jurisprudence of the European Court will be examined and then compared with the approach of the English courts.

CNTA

The *CNTA* case arose in the context of monetary compensatory amounts, a system introduced in agricultural sectors in the 1970s. The purpose of compensatory amounts was to compensate for the different price levels of agricultural produce resulting from the difference in exchange rates for national currencies.[115] Since currency fluctuations could result in a higher or lower monetary price being ascribed to a product than its real value, compensatory amounts were introduced to remedy such distortion. By allowing Member States to charge compensatory amounts on imports, and grant them on exports, the

---

[114] *CNTA*, above at n. 19, 559 (col. 1).

[115] See, generally, J.A. Usher, "Agricultural Markets: Their Price-Systems and Financial Mechanisms" (1979) 4 *EL Rev.* 147; F. Snyder, *Law of the Common Agricultural Policy* (Sweet & Maxwell, London, 1985), 111–21.

Community sought to keep the value of the products constant regardless of the currency in which it was expressed. Within this conflict between the need constantly to readjust compensatory amounts and the need for traders to have security in their transactions the principle of legitimate expectations was invoked.

The applicant had sought advance fixing of the compensatory amount refunds for the export of colza seeds, subject to a deposit, and had contracted to export the products. However, before the goods were exported the Commission abolished the applicable compensatory amounts for that sector.[116] The applicant claimed a legitimate expectation that the compensatory amounts would continue for deliveries in progress and that any losses suffered would be compensated for. The European Court acknowledged that the grant of an export licence fixing the refund amounts, subject to a deposit, could induce an expectation that no unforeseeable alteration would occur which would re-expose the trader to the exchange risk. The Court also held that in the absence of an overriding public interest the Commission should have adopted transitional measures to protect the applicant.

The balance between public and private interests was examined by Advocate General Trabucchi. The Advocate-General accepted that it was dangerous to lay down any general answer to how the Community should balance the competing interests or adopt appropriate measures in order to protect the expectations it had created. The balancing of the respective interests would always be determined by their specific nature and context. The regulation abolishing the applicable compensatory amounts stated that they were no longer necessary because 84% of Community production had either been sold or was in the process of being sold. The purpose of the compensatory amounts had been to protect the Community market by preventing agricultural prices from being compromised. The Commission had reasoned that as only 16% of the market remained, this did not present a threat to the Community and therefore abolished the applicable amounts. However, of that 84% of production 30% was regarded as committed for sale but had not yet been delivered to the purchaser. If the compensatory amounts were to be abolished this would affect that 30% yet to be delivered since the amounts were paid only on delivery. The applicant was in the position of having agreed to export his production on the basis that compensatory amounts would be payable on delivery. The Commission had done nothing to meet the expectations of those traders, such as the applicant, within the 30% band. It had placed support on the fact that this 30% of production had effectively left the home market in order to conclude that the same percentage should not have the benefit of the compensatory amounts. Advocate-General Trabucchi considered that there was a discernible inconsistency between the underlying reason for the abolition of the amounts and the fact that no account had been taken of the 30% of production which was an important element in the build up of the economic situation leading to the decision to

---

[116] Regulation No. 189/72 (OJ 1972 L24/25).

abolish the amounts.[117] The Commission's decision appeared to have "little in common with the principles of fair dealing and good faith which should govern the attitude of a public authority towards those subject to its control".[118] Consequently, the applicant's expectations were worthy of protection.

In this case, the underlying basis for the disappointment of the applicant's expectations was examined and an inconsistency was discovered. The public interest which the Commission argued compelled the expectations to be overridden was predicated upon a misconception: that the infringement of expectations was justified by a measure which, in fact, ignored the special position of those such as the applicant. In light of this inconsistency the public interest could not override the applicant's legitimate expectations. In this case it can be seen that the administrative court was prepared to inquire into the reasons put forward for the measure and examine whether in fact they required the disappointment of the individual's expectations.

Dürbeck

In *Dürbeck*[119] the European Court held that the public interest required the applicant's expectation to be overridden. The applicant had concluded contracts for the importation of Chilean apples and was in the process of transportation. However, the Commission temporarily suspended all imports of such apples into the Community. This measure was adopted because the imports threatened the sector with serious disturbances that could have endangered the objectives of the Common Agricultural Policy.[120] The applicant claimed that its expectations had been infringed because the Commission had failed to adopt any transitional measures to take account of traders with goods in transit. The European Court held that in light of the needs which the temporary suspension of imports met, the adoption of transitional measures "would have robbed the protective measure of all practical effect by opening the Community market in desert apples to a volume of imports likely to jeopardise that market".[121] Transitional measures would have defeated the purpose of the temporary suspension of imports. In the absence of alternative means to achieve the public interest the applicant's expectation had to give way.

---

[117] Ibid., 560 (col. 2).

[118] Ibid., 560 (col. 1) of the Advocate-General's opinion.

[119] Case 112/80 *Firma Anton Dürbeck* v. *Hauptzollamt Frankfurt am Main-Flughafen* [1981] ECR 1095.

[120] See Art. 33 of the EC Treaty.

[121] Dürbeck, above at n. 119, para. 50. See also Case 78/77 *Firma Johann Lührs* v. *Hauptzollamt Hamburg-Jonas* [1977] ECR 169; Case 127/78 *Hans Spitta & Co.* v. *Hauptzollamt Frankfurt am Main-Ost* [1979] ECR 171.

Spagl

The *Spagl* case[122] demonstrates the lengths to which the European Court will go to ensure that expectations are protected as far as possible. This dispute concerned the new provisions on milk quotas adopted after the *Mulder* ruling. The Community had adopted two measures in order to give protection to the expectations of those milk producers who had made a non-marketing undertaking and to meet the general interests of the Community in reducing the surplus of milk production. The applicant had made an undertaking to suspend his production and had been refused a reference quantity. On the basis of the expectations recognised in *Mulder*, i.e. that producers who had made an undertaking would not be treated any differently as a result, the applicant challenged the new measures on two grounds.

The first question concerned whether the Community could introduce a cut-off date for the grant of a special reference quantity. The new provisions stated that producers whose period of non-marketing ended before 31 December 1983 or 20 September 1983 could be refused the grant of a special reference quantity.[123] The applicant argued that this cut-off period infringed his expectations as it specifically affected him precisely because he had made the undertaking ending during the cut-off period. The Council and Commission argued that the public interest required the insertion of a cut-off date since the effectiveness of the system could be impaired by encouraging other producers to resume production who would not have otherwise done so but who wished to profit from the precious asset of a milk quota. The European Court rejected this argument: the cut-off date could not be justified by reasons relating to the public interest as that could alternatively be safeguarded by measures of a general nature. If the general interest required a restriction to the scheme, that objective would have been better served by a measure of general application rather than specific restrictions which affected producers precisely because they had made a non-marketing undertaking.

The second question concerned whether the special reference quantity provided for producers who had made an undertaking could be restricted to 60% of the quantity of milk delivered by the producer in the twelve months preceding the undertaking. As such producers had produced no milk during the chosen reference year some other form of calculation had to be devised in order to determine the special reference quantity they were to be given. The method used was to take a representative period before the undertaking, from which a reduction of 40% was to be made to ensure that those producers were not accorded an undue advantage compared with other producers. This reduction was also challenged as an infringement of legitimate expectations. The European Court held that the principle precluded the reduction rate being fixed at such a high

---

[122] Case C–189/89 *Spagl* v. *Hauptzollamt Rosenheim* [1990] ECR I–4539. See also Case C–217/89 *Pastätter* v. *Hauptzollamt Bad Reichenhall* [1990] ECR I–4585.

[123] Regulation No. 764/89 (OJ 1989 L84/2), which amended Regulation No. 857/84.

level for producers who had made an undertaking. Having obtained information from the Commission the Court found that the reduction rates applicable to producers who had not made an undertaking did not exceed 17.5%.[124] Therefore, the 40% reduction was over twice the highest reduction for the other producers and this difference in treatment specifically affected producers because they had made a non-marketing undertaking.

In response the Council and Commission claimed that it was not possible to give such producers special reference quantities of more than 60% of their milk deliveries without undermining the objective of the scheme to deal with structural surpluses in the milk market. The Commission estimated that one million tonnes of milk would be covered by the requests for the grant of a special reference quantity, whereas the Council considered that 600,000 tonnes of milk was the largest volume compatible with the objectives of the scheme. The Community reserve had been increased by 600,000 tonnes and the reference quantities of other producers remained unchanged. In other words, the producers who had made the undertaking were getting as much as was considered possible without undermining the purpose of the whole scheme. However, the European Court found that this public interest did not compel the disappointment of the applicants' expectations. Even if a larger increase than the Community reserve could not be contemplated without the risk of disturbing the balance of the milk market, an alternative existed to the 60% rule. The Community could have reduced the reference quantities of the other producers proportionately by a corresponding amount so as to enable the allocation of larger reference quantities to the producers who had made the undertaking. It was possible to lower the reference quantities as a whole in order to spread the necessary reduction throughout the whole sector rather than specifically to target producers who had made an undertaking.

To summarise this judgment, it may be said that the European Court was concerned to ensure that the applicants' expectations were protected as far as possible and undertook a close examination of the balance between the competing interests. The Court rejected any other restrictions placed on the producers because the public interest objective of those restrictions could have been achieved by alternative measures. The tenor of the ruling was that all producers should be similarly affected by any restriction made in the general interest and not just those producers who had made an undertaking. What is so striking about the case is how closely the European Court was prepared to advance an alternative course which required the reprocessing of all reference quantities in order to protect the legitimate expectations of a certain class of producer. In weighing up the competing interests, the European Court sought to maximise protection of the individual's expectation in light of the Community goal to reduce surplus milk production.

---

[124] The 17.5% reduction was the highest reduction applicable for any producer awarded a reference quantity following a chosen reference year and had been made by the United Kingdom; see para. 43 of Advocate-General Jacobs' opinion.

From this examination of the European Court's case law, the following comments may be made. The European Court adopts a goal-oriented review to determine whether an expectation is worthy of protection. The balancing exercise is based upon the assumption that law is a necessary feature of the administrative process. The European Court does not take a subsidiary role in examining whether the administration has exceeded the limits of what was reasonable. Its role is to optimise the individual's expectation to the extent that the achievement of the public purpose remains factually possible. The Court will examine whether the infringement of the expectation was indispensable for the achievement of the public interest objective by looking at all the relevant circumstances and the availability of alternative measures. The cases demonstrate that the nature of administrative adjudication inevitably involves not just judging the administration but also actively engaging in administrative processes. In determining the legitimacy of expectations the European Court performs this task by promoting policy objectives constructively and advising on the forms of implementation needed to protect expectations.

Hamble and *Hargreaves*

What method have the English courts adopted for determining the legitimacy of an expectation? Parker L.J. acknowledged that once an individual has claimed an expectation the public authority may argue that an overriding public interest exists which requires the expectation to be disappointed.[125] However, the problem for English courts has been the question of precisely who is to decide whether the public interest overrides the individual's expectation. Is the public authority to be the sole judge of what are the requirements of the public interest and also whether the achievement of that goal requires the individual's expectation to be sacrificed? Or is the court to examine the balance struck by the public authority? If so, how is the court to undertake such a review? Is it to weigh the competing interests itself, or should it adopt the customary approach of *Wednesbury* unreasonableness? Disagreement over the appropriate test for determining the legitimacy of an expectation and the acceptable limits of judicial review has arisen recently between Sedley J. and the Court of Appeal.

The *Hamble* case[126] concerned the transfer of licences for vessels fishing for pressure stocks of fish protected by European Community quotas. Each Member State had been allocated a quota for such stocks and had to determine the detailed rules for their application. In the United Kingdom this was achieved by the issue of licences for fishing vessels. Section 4 of the Sea Fish (Conservation) Act 1967 made it a criminal offence for any British registered vessel to fish without a licence. In order to grant the licences a policy had been

---

[125] *Khan*, above at n. 58, 46b, 48f.
[126] *Hamble*, above at n. 53.

adopted. Each vessel was given a vessel capacity unit (VCU) to be determined by its size and engine power. The transfer of licences from one vessel to another was permissible provided the total VCU of an operator's fleet was not increased. Under the policy permitting the transfer of pressure stock licences from one boat to another, the applicant had purchased a vessel, the *Nellie*. The applicant later purchased two other vessels with beam trawl licences in order to aggregate these licences together for the *Nellie*. However, the Ministry subsequently announced a moratorium on the aggregation of licences to reduce the pressure on fish stocks. The applicant claimed a legitimate expectation that any change in policy would not frustrate the completion of the process of licence aggregation for the *Nellie*.

One preliminary point must be noted here. Sedley J. accepted that although the case arose under a domestic statute, it would be unrealistic to treat the point of law as entirely domestic. The purpose of the legislation was to allow the Ministry to implement and give effect to the Common Fisheries Policy. A major part of this policy would be frustrated if, in the implementation of the policy, the Member State was governed only by its national law. Furthermore, the possibility of a preliminary reference to the European Court required the national court to have full regard to European jurisprudence.[127] Sedley J. therefore proceeded to define the principle of legitimate expectations by reference to the case law of the European Court.[128]

Following this review Sedley J. sought to identify "the legal alchemy which gives an expectation sufficient legitimacy to secure enforcement in public law".[129] The judge stated that "legitimacy is itself a relative concept, to be gauged proportionately to the legal and policy implications of the expectation".[130] He continued:[131]

> "Legitimacy in this sense is not an absolute. It is a function of expectations induced by government and policy considerations which militate against their fulfilment. The balance must in the first instance be for the policy-maker to strike; but if the outcome is challenged by way of judicial review, I do not consider that the court's criterion is the bare rationality of the policy-maker's conclusion. While policy is for the policy-maker alone, the fairness of his or her decision not to accommodate reasonable expectations which the policy will thwart remains the court's concern."

The legitimacy of an expectation was to be determined by balancing the needs of protecting it against the public policy considerations. Sedley J. denied that this placed the court in the seat of the minister:[132]

---

[127] That *Hamble* was a case which fell to be decided under European Community principles of law is supported by the subsequent classification drawn in R. v. *Ministry of Agriculture, Fisheries and Food, ex parte First City Trading Ltd.* [1997] 1 CMLR. 250, 269.

[128] Reference was made to the various cases of the European Court examined in this ch. and also to Schwarze, above at n. 2, 867–8.

[129] *Hamble*, above at n. 53, 728j.

[130] Ibid., 724c.

[131] Ibid., 731c–d.

[132] Ibid., 731d–e.

"[I]t is the court's task to recognise the constitutional importance of ministerial freedom to formulate and to reformulate policy; but it is equally the court's duty to protect the interests of those individuals whose expectation of different treatment has a
legitimacy which in fairness outtops the policy choice which threatens to frustrate it."

The clearly expressed judgment of Sedley J. signalled that the English courts
should undertake a balancing act in the same manner as the European Court.
Legitimate expectation was now a term of art reserved for those expectations
which were not only reasonable but which could be sustained by the court in the
face of a policy change. As the judge stated, it was for the court to determine
whether the expectation was legitimate. The implication from the judgment is
that English courts should not adopt a differential approach in determining the
legitimacy of an expectation. European case law was drawn upon as a means of
refining the meaning of the principle in English law. In this process of assimilating the principle in both English and Community law the *Hamble* decision represents one of the most explicit cases to date to recognise that principles of
judicial review are no longer self-contained within national legal systems.
English courts can no longer develop principles of law without reference to similar principles in European law.

On the facts of the case Sedley J. refused the application. The course of licence
aggregation was far from complete and the change of policy would not destroy
the investment made completely. The fulfilment of the applicant's expectation
would have prevented the change of policy. Once it was accepted that it was not
legitimate to expect that a policy would not be changed, the expectation was little more than a hope. Furthermore, the exclusion of the applicant from transitional provisions was not unfair because if the minister had taken account of the
applicant's expectations it might well have eventually subverted the policy.

While the *Hamble* case was praised for its understanding of European
jurisprudence, it was soon criticised for advancing a wrong and irresponsible
proposition of law. In a speech reaffirming the need for the courts to maintain
their traditional restraint towards public decisions and apply the *Wednesbury*
standard of review, Lord Irvine stated that the approach adopted in *Hamble*
was "no more than judicial irredentism":[133]

"[I]t is to advance from a hard-edged decision on the existence and extent of a legitimate expectation (which is proper) to a hard-edged review of the merits of the
Secretary of State's overall decision as to whether that legitimate expectation may be
overridden (which is improper)."

The notion that the court should undertake a balancing exercise would
exceed the limits placed upon judicial review. The only role that the court could
legitimately exercise was deciding whether the failure to take account of an indi-

---

[133] Lord Irvine of Lairg QC, "Judges and Decision-Makers: The Theory and Practice of
Wednesbury Review" [1996] *PL* 59, 72. See also Lord Irvine of Lairg QC, "Recent Developments in
Public Law in the United Kingdom" (The Singapore Academy of Law Annual Lecture 1999), at
http://www.open.gov.uk/lcd/speeches/1999/1999fr.htm.

vidual's expectation was not unreasonable. If the court exercised any further review it would be substituting its view for that of the decision-maker and therefore transgressing the boundary between appeal and review.

This line of argument also found favour with the Court of Appeal which had the opportunity in *Hargreaves*,[134] a case concerning a change in sentencing policy, to respond to the approach developed in *Hamble*. Hirst L.J. emphatically dismissed the notion of a balancing exercise:[135]

"[Counsel] . . . characterised Sedley J's approach as heresy, and in my judgment he was right to do so. On matters of substance (as contrasted with procedure) *Wednesbury* provides the correct test."

Pill L.J. understood Sedley J. to have been making "[t]he claim to a broader power to judge the fairness of a decision of substance . . . [which was] . . . wrong in principle".[136] Rather than merely distinguishing *Hamble* as a case decided under the scope of Community law, the Court of Appeal emphatically denounced and overruled the approach taken there. The carefully reasoned and prepared *Hamble* judgment, which had undertaken an extensive review of the principle, was dismissed by employing the rhetorical force of "heresy".[137] The judges considered that if the court were to review the balance struck by the decision-maker and examine whether the objective behind the policy change could be achieved without extinguishing the applicant's expectation, it would be examining the intrinsic merits of the policy decision itself. This was beyond the limits of the judicial role set by time-hallowed reference to *Wednesbury* unreasonableness.

There are compelling reasons to support the view that the Court of Appeal's rejection of the balancing exercise was misconceived.[138] Determining the legitimacy of an expectation inevitably involves striking some balance between the competing interests. The court can do this either through an explicit balancing process or by using the customary language of *Wednesbury* unreasonableness. The question is always whether the individual's expectation can be accommodated within the policy change made by the public authority. As the case law of the European Court demonstrates, no general guidance can be laid down for this task because the goals of public administration change. It is for the administrative court to determine the extent of the applicant's expectation in light of such changes. In contrast, the response of the Court of Appeal evinces a self-deception and an inability to engage in this inquiry constructively.

---

[134] *Hargreaves*, above at n. 63.

[135] Ibid., 412H.

[136] Ibid., 416c.

[137] Cf. T. Hobbes, *Leviathan* [1651] (University Press, Oxford, 1996), ch. XI, section 19: "men give different names, to one and the same thing, from the difference of their own passions: as they that approve a private opinion, call it opinion; but they that mislike it, heresy: and yet heresy signifies no more than private opinion; but has only a greater tincture of choler [anger]".

[138] See P.P. Craig, "Substantive Legitimate Expectations and the Principles of Judicial Review", in *The Common Law of Europe and the Public Law of the United Kingdom* (King's College, London, SPTL Seminar, 14 June 1997), 11.

The self-deception was that the court was not itself undertaking the "heretical" balancing exercise under a different guise. Despite protestations to the contrary, the use of the unreasonableness test itself necessarily involves the balancing of competing interests, but not on any rational or explicit basis. The invocation of *Wednesbury* does not resolve such issues automatically; in reality, it obfuscates them. This tautological definition of unreasonableness, indicative of the anti-rationalist traditions of common law, allows the courts to think that they are not undertaking a balancing exercise even though, on any rational interpretation, that is precisely what is called for. It allows the judges to avoid, or rather never think through, a more rational and explicit justification for their decision. In this sense, the casuistic unreasonableness test is actually more dangerous than the balancing exercise because it can act as a cloak for the courts' social and economic preferences.[139] The Court of Appeal was simply incapable of providing any rational or constructive guidance as to how the administration should assess the legitimacy of an expectation.

In contrast with the balancing of interests undertaken by the European Court, English courts are reluctant to adopt a similar approach for fear of examining the merits of public decisions. While the English courts have recognised that public administration "extends not to a single case but to the management of a continuing regime",[140] they have not adequately considered whether their own task extends merely to the single case or to the management of a continuing regime. Instead of developing the principle as a means of guiding and structuring the exercise of public power by elaborating and rationalising how the administration should balance the competing interests, the courts have preferred the highly particular *Wednesbury* test, which is the complete antithesis of a rational guidance mechanism. The reason for this is that the underlying thought of English administrative law has been unable adequately to incorporate a developed principle of public law. The rule-oriented jurisprudence cannot accommodate the pragmatic balancing of interests. How can the courts effectively protect expectations if they maintain the distinction between adjudication and administration? The answer is that they cannot, except in superficial terms. English judges do not view themselves as having a constructive role in policy implementation, and retreat into customary doctrine to avoid it. While the courts recognise the importance of legal certainty for individuals, they cannot provide any rational or constructive guidance as to how the administration should respect expectations. Laws J. has acknowledged that "[l]egitimate expectations is no more an absolute doctrine in Europe than in England".[141] However, this does little to address the critical issue of the different underlying conceptions of the role of law in government.

---

[139] J. Jowell and A. Lester, "Beyond *Wednesbury*: Substantive Principles of Administrative Law" [1987] *PL* 368, 381.

[140] *Southwark*, above at n. 77, 320E.

[141] *R. v. Secretary of State for Health, ex parte Macrae Seafoods Ltd.* (1995) unreported 12 June, QBD.

The condemnation of the balancing test by the Court of Appeal is therefore more expressive of that court's own conception of legality rather than the extent to which any expectations are worthy of protection. Again, the limited dualisms—procedure and substance, legality and merits, appeal and review—pervade the legal discourse and obscure the issues involved. It is submitted that the response of the Court of Appeal in *Hargreaves* demonstrates a failure to understand a developed principle of administrative justice. In light of the impact of Community law discussed earlier[142] the Court of Appeal missed an opportunity to adopt a constructive approach to the differentiation of legal standards between English and Community law.[143]

LIABILITY

To what extent can an individual receive compensation for losses arising from a breach of legitimate expectations? Article 215(2) of the EC Treaty provides that the Community shall, in accordance with the general principles of law, make good any damage for which it is responsible. As regards legislative acts involving choices of economic policy the Community will be liable only if it has committed a sufficiently serious breach of a superior rule of law.[144] Losses caused by a breach of legitimate expectations can give rise to damages if there was a manifest and sufficiently serious breach. In *Sofrimport SARL* v. *Commission*[145] the Commission had infringed the legitimate expectations of traders with goods in transit by adopting protective measures prohibiting such goods from entering the Community. The European Court held that the Commission had completely failed to take account of the position of such traders who had suffered losses beyond the economic risks inherent in their business. Furthermore, there was no overriding public interest to justify the disappointment of such expectations. The Commission had therefore committed a sufficiently serious violation of the principle.

This decision can be contrasted with the second *Mulder* case[146] in which milk producers sought damages arising from the total and permanent exclusion from the milk market and the more limited exclusion following the adoption of the 60% rule. As regards the total and permanent exclusion, which had been dealt with in the first *Mulder* case, the European Court held that there had been a

---

[142]   See ch. 2.

[143]   In a subsequent case, *R.* v. *North and East Devon Health Authority, ex parte Coughlan* (1999) unreported, 16 July, the Court of Appeal, composed of Lord Woolf M.R., Mummery L.J. and Sedley L.J., reiterated the approach advanced in *Hamble*.

[144]   Case 5/71 *Aktien-Zuckerfabrik Schöppenstedt* v. *Council* [1971] ECR 975. See, generally, T. Heukels and A. MacDonnell (eds), *The Action for Damages in Community Law* (Kluwer, London, 1997); P.P. Craig and G. de Búrca, *EU Law: Text, Cases and Materials* (Clarendon Press, Oxford, 2nd ed. 1998), ch. 12.

[145]   Case C–152/88 [1990] ECR I–2477.

[146]   Joined Cases C–104/89 and 37/90, *Mulder* v. *Council and Commission* [1992] ECR I–3061.

manifest breach of legitimate expectations. The Community had failed to take account of those producers who had made a non-marketing undertaking without invoking any higher public interest. This failure was all the more evident because the exclusion from the market had been unforeseeable and had exceeded the normal risks inherent in the market. The Community was therefore liable to compensate losses arising from the total and permanent exclusion. However, the limited exclusion arising from the rule that reference quantities of such producers would be 60% of their deliveries in the year before they undertook not to produce milk, declared unlawful in *Spagl*, did not amount to a sufficiently serious violation for two reasons. First, the rule did, to an extent, allow the producers to resume their activities. Therefore, the Community had not failed to take account of their situation completely. Secondly, the rule was a choice of economic policy made in pursuance of a higher public interest. The margin of error afforded to the Community had not been exceeded because the rule served the higher public interest of seeking to reduce the milk surplus. The total exclusion from the market had been unforeseeable and inexcusable, whereas the limited exclusion under the 60% rule had attempted to strike a more appropriate balance.

The position in English law is very different because of the lack of any principle of administrative liability. Public authorities are subject to the same rules as private individuals. To be compensated for any losses arising from a disappointment of expectation an individual must found a suitable action in tort or contract. This limited range of remedies for public law action in England contrasts sharply with Continental ideas of administrative liability.[147] The only possibilities available to an individual would be either an action for negligent mis-statement or misfeasance in a public office. Since the requirement to take account of legitimate expectations is not considered to be a statutory obligation, an action for breach of statutory duty will not be available. Another possibility is the award of an *ex gratia* payment by the administration following an investigation for maladministration by the Parliamentary Commissioner for Administration.[148] The lack of a specific remedy for governmental liability in English law compares unfavourably with the position in European law.

CONCLUSION

In this chapter the development of legitimate expectations in English and European Community law has been compared. Whereas the European Court has effectively employed the principle, the English judiciary has experienced uncertainty and confusion over its role, scope and meaning. It is submitted that

---

[147] See, e.g., L. Neville Brown and J.S. Bell with the assistance of J.-M. Galabert, *French Administrative Law* (Clarendon Press, Oxford, 5th ed. 1998), ch. 8.
[148] See A.R. Mowbray, "A Right to Official Advice: The Parliamentary Commissioner's Perspective" [1990] *PL* 68.

an explanation can be found in the different underlying approaches to the role of law in government. For the European Court, law provides a means of ensuring that the policy objectives of the Community are both effectively and equitably achieved. By contrast, English courts do not accept that this is something with which they ought to concern themselves. The consequence is that they have experienced difficulty in handling the principle. The underlying difference between the conceptions of administrative law here has rarely been acknowledged but explains the divergence of approach. Assessments that English and European law have "in very broad terms marched hand in hand as regards legitimate expectation"[149] or that there is "a common tendency to check unfairness"[150] merely conceal such differences.

Perhaps the biggest difficulty for the English judiciary is that the principle requires them to perform a different role in realising expectations in light of the changing demands of public administration. Administrative courts are concerned with promoting administrative policies by resolving disputes. This approach requires the judiciary to have the necessary institutional confidence and knowledge of governmental processes to apply the principle. At present, English courts appear uncertain. For example, in the *Spagl* case the European Court required a reorganisation of all the reference quantities for milk quotas in order to protect the applicants' expectations. The most that English courts have required is for the Home Secretary to exempt an individual from the application of a policy.[151] They have also allowed the Home Secretary an almost unfettered discretion to change sentencing policy without regard to prisoners' expectations.[152]

In 1978 J.D.B. Mitchell noted that in applying the principle of legitimate expectation the European Court had demonstrated "a sense of administrative morality". By contrast, English cases illustrate the way in which "the underlying thought of British administrative law . . . [has] . . . failed to adjust to the problem of modern government".[153] While English courts have enhanced the protection of individuals' expectations in government, they have been unable to enforce an administrative morality effectively. The protection of substantive expectations and the balancing of interests have troubled the courts. Furthermore, English law lacks any remedy of compensation against the administration.

---

[149] Laws, above at n. 47, 2.
[150] Lord Mackenzie Stuart, "Legitimate Expectations and Estoppel in Community Law and English Administrative Law" [1983/1] *Legal Issues of European Integration* 53, 73.
[151] *Khan*, above at n. 58.
[152] *Findlay*, above at n. 57; *Hargreaves*, above at n. 63.
[153] J.D.B. Mitchell, "Law, Democracy and Political Institutions", in M Cappelletti (ed.), *New Perspectives For a Common Law of Europe* (Sijthoff, Leyden, 1978), 361, 373.

4

Proportionality (I): European Doctrine and English Debate

P ROPORTIONALITY CONCERNS THE relationship between the ends of public action and the means used to attain them. To achieve its objectives the administration must adopt effective means of policy implementation since the justification for the very existence of public administration is to realise collective goals through programmes of state action. In so doing the administration may adversely affect the interests of a private individual. It would be an impossible task for the administration to fulfil social needs and avoid any such interference. Clearly, private interests have to be subordinated to the greater public good. However, it may be argued that the extent of the interference was unnecessary since the public goal could have been achieved through different means. The role of the administrative court in applying proportionality is to examine the effectiveness of such alternative courses of action in light of the administration's objective. If there are alternative means, less restrictive of the individual's interests but equally effective for the realisation of the public objective, then the interference is unnecessary and disproportionate. The determination of the proportionality of a public measure requires the administrative court to formulate judicial opinions concerning policy implementation. It undertakes a goal-oriented balancing exercise to establish whether it was factually possible for the administration to use alternative means. Proportionality is therefore a key tool of modern administrative law to ensure the purposive rationality of public action.

This chapter will examine and compare the use of proportionality in European and English law. Proportionality has long been accepted as a principle of European law, whereas in England it still awaits formal recognition. However, this has not prevented a vigorous debate over its "possible adoption".[1] In examining this debate this chapter will bring to light the different styles of public law thought as they are integral to judicial and academic discourse. What follows is an attempt to understand the principle by recognising the different conceptions of what "administrative law" is. It seeks to demonstrate that the specific meaning attributed to proportionality is contingent upon assumptions concerning the role of law in public administration.

---

[1] *Council of Civil Service Unions* v. *Minister for the Civil Service* [1985] AC 374, 410E. See also *Hansard*, H.L. Deb., Vol. 379, cols 993–4, 3 February 1977.

Verhältnismäßigkeit (proportionality) originates from German public law where it developed not as an implied legislative prohibition against the unreasonable exercise of power but on a more fundamental and scientific basis of ends and means or cause and effect relationship.[2] The importance of subjecting administrative discretion to law has required German administrative courts to play an essential role in the achievement of tasks in the administrative state. Review of the proportionality of public decision-making requires the administration to adopt suitable measures having the capacity to further its aim. Furthermore, intervention by the state must not go beyond what is necessary in the circumstances.[3] The extensive ability of administrative courts to find facts, and their specialist jurisdiction, enables them rationalise the impact of public decisions on individuals. As German jurists have emphasised, one of the most important features of administrative law is to ensure that administrative authorities act with sensitivity towards individuals. Proportionality is therefore an important principle of state action.

Having adapted the principle from German law, the European Court applies proportionality across the range of Community activities.[4] As Advocate-General Jacobs noted, there are few areas of Community law where the principle is not relevant.[5] Proportionality is pre-eminent in the Court's review of legality and has been written into the European Treaties.[6] According to Advocate-General Dutheillet de Lamothe, proportionality in public administration requires that "citizens may only have imposed on them, for the purposes of the public interest, obligations which are strictly necessary for those purposes to be attained".[7] In a more recent formulation the European Court articulated proportionality in terms of its three constituent tests of suitability, necessity and proportionality in the narrow sense:[8]

---

[2] L. Hirschberg, *Der Grundsatz der Verhältnismäßigkeit* (Göttingen, 1981), 43–4, quoted in M.P. Singh, *German Administrative Law in Common Law Perspective* (Springer-Verlag, Berlin, 1985), 88. See also N. Emiliou, *The Principle of Proportionality in European Law: A Comparative Study* (Kluwer, London, 1996), ch. 2. On proportionality in French administrative law, see ibid., ch. 3; L. Neville Brown and J.S. Bell with the assistance of J.-M. Galabert, *French Administrative Law* (Clarendon Press, Oxford, 1998), 233–5, 261–7.

[3] See G. Nolte, "General Principles of German and European Administrative Law—A Comparison in Historical Perspective" (1994) 57 *MLR* 191, 193.

[4] See, generally, J. Schwarze, *European Administrative Law* (Sweet & Maxwell, London, 1992), ch. 5; G. de Búrca, "The Principle of Proportionality and its Application in EC Law" (1993) 13 *Yearbook of European Law* 105; Emiliou, above at n. 2.

[5] Case C–120/94 *Commission* v. *Greece* [1996] ECR 1513, 1533, para. 70 of the Advocate-General's opinion.

[6] See Art. 5 of the EC Treaty.

[7] Case 11/70 *Internationale Handelsgesellschaft* v. *Einfuhr- und Vorratsstelle* [1970] ECR 1125, 1146 (col. 1) of the Advocate-General's opinion.

[8] Case C–331/88 R. v. *Ministry of Agriculture, Fisheries and Food, ex parte Fedesa* [1990] ECR I–4023, para. 13.

"By virtue of that principle, the lawfulness of the prohibition of an economic activity is subject to the condition that the prohibitory measures are appropriate and necessary in order to achieve the objectives legitimately pursued by the legislation in question; when there is a choice between several appropriate measures recourse must be had to the least onerous, and the disadvantages caused must not be disproportionate to the aims pursued."

Since the principle is so widely applied, uncertainty has arisen over its precise scope. In some cases the European Court states that the impugned measure will be disproportionate only if it is "manifestly inappropriate" in light of its objective,[9] whereas in other cases the Court will scrutinise the content of the measure closely. It is apparent that the principle operates on a sliding scale of review. The conception of legality required by the Court will vary in light of the context of the particular policy objective, the nature of the competing interests involved and the competence of the Court to make certain evaluative findings concerning the implementation of policy objectives. The specific framework of review in which the Court articulates the principle is set at varying levels of intensity in light of such factors. As Advocate-General Capotorti has intimated, an infringement of proportionality will not be held to have occurred "without careful reflection on the scope of that principle and on the importance which the facts given assume in its light".[10] Deciding which framework of review best expresses the requirement of proportionality is an essential feature in its application. Broadly speaking, three types of case can be discerned: where the challenged measure concerns a choice of economic policy, affects Treaty or fundamental rights or imposes a penalty.

Economic policy measures

The European Community was established for the purpose of integration in order to promote competition in order to improve economic performance. To ensure that the market functions effectively Community institutions have powers to intervene to correct imbalances and orient economic development in accordance with general Community objectives. Such intervention in the economic sphere is bound to impact upon individuals and traders. To ensure that the process of economic integration does not undermine the freedom necessary for its success there must be some check on the method of policy implementation. Proportionality enables the Court to determine whether such intervention is capable of achieving its aims and to ensure that it goes no further than is necessary. According to J. Mertens de Wilmars, a former judge at the European Court, from the economic point of view the principle of proportionality embodies two concepts fundamental to democratic mixed-economy systems: that

---

[9] Ibid., para. 14.

[10] Joined Cases 154, 205, 206, 226–228, 263 and 264/78, 39, 31, 83 and 85/79 *SpA Ferriera Valsabbia* v. *Commission* [1980] ECR 9007, 1055 (col. 2) of the Advocate-General's opinion.

public intervention must be subsidiary in nature and that there must be a connection between an intervention threshold and the safeguard of individual liberties.[11] The level, depth and extent of intervention must be examined to ensure that it does not undermine the objective of promoting an open market economy with free competition. Since measures of economic intervention are usually of a general normative nature, it is inevitable that certain interests will be adversely affected in some way. The competing interests are so generalised and multifarious that the review exercised by the Court must take account of this. Community institutions are under no obligation to avoid decisions which adversely affect any interests. However, the institutions should avoid harmful consequences for those affected by a measure if alternative means are available.

Germany v. *Council (Bananas)*[12] demonstrates how the European Court will adopt a marginal review limited to examining whether the measure is manifestly disproportionate. The case concerned a challenge to a Council regulation[13] which introduced a new common organisation of the market in bananas. Prior to its adoption the Community has been supplied by bananas produced in the Community, those produced in countries which had signed the Lomé Convention (the ACP States) and those produced in third countries. The regulation introduced common quality and marketing controls which favoured Community importers of bananas from the ACP States, mostly French, Spanish and Portugeuse businesses, but prejudiced importers from third country producers, which were largely German undertakings. The German Government argued that the tariff quota imposed on third country imports placed excessive burdens on certain traders and was not necessary. The European Court rejected the argument that the Council had acted disproportionately. In adopting the regulation the Council had been required to reconcile divergent interests and to ensure the marketing of products at reasonable prices. The Council had also been required to determine the system's future effects, which depended on a series of factors, such as consumer reaction, which were difficult to foresee. The regulation would be invalidated only on the basis that the Council had made manifestly incorrect assessments of the assumptions and effects involved in its policy choice. In the present case the Council had not made any manifest error in its choice of means to be overruled by the Court within the framework of its review of legality.[14]

While the European Court typically adopts this stringent test of legality, it will hold a measure to be invalid if it is excessively disproportionate compared

---

[11] J. Mertens de Wilmars, "The Case-Law of the Court of Justice in Relation to the Review of the Legality of Economic Policy in Mixed-Economy Systems" [1982/1] *Legal Issues of European Integration* 1, 13.

[12] Case C–208/93 [1994] ECR I–4973.

[13] Regulation No. 404/93 (OJ 1993 L47/1).

[14] Paragraph 87 of Advocate-General Gulmann's opinion. On the subsequent case law of the German courts, see N. Reich, "Judge-made 'Europe à la carte': Some Remarks on Recent Conflicts between European and German Constitutional Law Provoked by the Banana Litigation" (1996) 7 *European Journal of International Law* 103.

with alternative courses of action. In the "skimmed-milk" case[15] the Court annulled a Council regulation on this basis. The Community had been faced with an increasing surplus of skimmed-milk powder and had adopted a regulation to reduce this surplus by increasing its use in animal feed. The regulation made grants of Community aid for producers of animal feeding-stuffs conditional upon the purchase of quantities of skimmed-milk at a price that was three times its value as animal feed. The Court invalidated this measure because it imposed a disproportionate burden on the producers of animal feed. The Council had sought to reduce the milk powder surplus but its method of achieving this goal had involved an excessive burden on producers from other sectors who were not responsible for the surplus. In the opinion of Advocate-General Capotorti, there were two possible courses of action open to the Council. First, the burden could have been distributed more evenly if it had been spread throughout the Community indirectly via the budget. Secondly, the costs of processing liquid skimmed-milk into powder was higher than the market price of the milk used in animal feed. Had the processing of liquid milk into powder been discouraged and devoted to other purposes it would have reduced the surplus. Compared with the advantage sought for the Community the system made excessive demands on certain categories of producers. The case demonstrates that if a measure imposes a particularly onerous burden and its objective could have been achieved through alternative means it will be to be invalidated on the grounds of proportionality.

Proportionality may also be used to promote the effective realisation of a policy goal. In *Mignini*[16] the Court invalidated a condition that producers of soya bean would receive aid only if their produce could be identified on the premises of their production establishment. The purpose of the aid was to promote soya bean production, but in order to avoid fraudulent claims it was necessary for producers to have storage facilities on their premises of production. The Court held that this condition could deter applications for aid and frustrate the whole purpose of the system. Since control of the system could have been achieved by other means, such as the approval of separate storage facilities, the condition had imposed an unnecessary requirement. Rather than questioning the aid policy, the Court's review was directed towards strengthening its effectiveness.

Measures affecting treaty and fundamental rights

The Common Market is based upon the four fundamental freedoms (free movement of goods, workers, establishment and services) which give positive economic rights to Community citizens. These Treaty rights have been accorded

---

[15] Case 114/76 *Bela-Mühle Josef Bergmann KG* v. *Grows-Farm GmbH & Co. KG* [1977] ECR 1211.
[16] Case C–256/90 *Mignini SpA* v. *Azienda di Stato per gli Interventi nel Mercato Agricolo (AIMA)* [1992] ECR I–2651.

great importance by the European Court in terms of how the Community affects the ordinary lives of its citizens and because they are central to the whole enterprise of economic integration. However, the rights are not absolute. The Treaty allows the Member States to derogate from them in a limited range of circumstances. Proportionality is used to review the extent of such derogations. Any limitation of such a right for a specific purpose must not go beyond what is necessary to achieve its objective. When examining the legality of a derogation the European Court will already have part of its evaluative framework in place as the importance accorded to the Treaty right is acknowledged. Proportionality is therefore applied with greater intensity in this context. For example, in a dispute concerning the importation of UHT milk into the United Kingdom the requirement of an import licence was held to be contrary to the free movement of goods.[17] The United Kingdom had established the system of import licence to prevent milk from diseased cattle entering the country. The issue of such licences depended upon administrative discretion and therefore created uncertainty for traders. The European Court held that public health could have been equally served if the authorities had obtained the relevant information by means of declarations signed by importers and, if necessary, accompanied by the appropriate certificates.

The European Court also uses proportionality to ensure that fundamental rights receive sufficient protection. This book is not the place to examine the jurisprudence of the European Court as regards fundamental rights.[18] In general terms it can be stated that while the Court recognises that those rights are not absolute, any restriction must correspond to general Community objectives and not constitute a disproportionate and intolerable interference with the substance of the rights. For example, in exercising its discretion in the implementation of Community rules the Member State should go no further than is necessary in interfering with fundamental rights.[19]

Measures imposing a penalty

Administrative decisions may impose a penalty upon individuals or traders to ensure compliance with Community law. Such decisions are reviewable if the penalty imposed is excessive. Unlike economic policy measures, the competing interests involved are usually specific. The individual's interest is in the degree of the penalty, while the Community interest is in ensuring that Community law is applied. In reviewing the proportionality of penalties the Court can promote its effectiveness for achieving its purpose and ensure that the individual or trader concerned does not suffer an excessive or disproportionate burden.

[17] Case 124/81 *Commission* v. *United Kingdom* [1983] ECR 203. See, further, Emiliou, above at n. 2, ch. 7.

[18] See, generally, P.P. Craig and G. de Búrca, *EU Law: Text, Cases and Materials* (Clarendon Press, Oxford, 2nd ed. 1998), ch. 7.

[19] Case 5/99 *Wachauf* v. *Bundesmat Für Ernährung und Forstwirtschaft* [1989] ECR 2609.

In the context of the Common Agricultural Policy, penalties, such as the forfeiture of deposits lodged by traders, may be imposed if the trader fails to fulfil its obligations.[20] The purpose of the system of deposits is to enable the Community to have a good idea of trade movements by reflecting real trade through the issue of licences subject to deposits. A deposit will be lost if the goods are not imported or exported according to the licence. In *Buitoni*[21] an importer of tomatoes had obtained import certificates for which a deposit had been lodged. However, the French intervention agency refused to return the deposit because the importer had failed to submit proof of importation within six months. The forfeiture of deposit was intended to guarantee importation, but had been imposed here due to the failure to submit proof of importation. The European Court held that to impose the same penalty for failure to submit proof of importation as for failure to import was excessively severe in relation to the objectives of administrative efficiency in the context of import and export levies. The charge should have been considerably less onerous and more closely connected with its practical effects. Similarly, in the *Man (Sugar)* case[22] the European Court held that the loss of a deposit of over £1.5 million was an excessive penalty to pay for the delayed application of an export licence, which was less than four hours late.

In these cases the European Court does not use the "marginal review" formula, but draws a tighter framework of review because of the different nature of the decision-making. The penalty is usually of an individual nature concerning one trader, rather than a decision requiring an overall assessment of the economic situation. The Court therefore adopts a more intensive review to ensure that penalties are proportionate to the maximum extent the smooth-running and efficiency of the deposit system allows.

Review for proportionality

Proportionality allows the Court to subject public measures to close scrutiny. For historical reasons the German courts are conscious of the potential arbitrariness of discretionary power and therefore subject public measures to intensive review to ensure that they are proportionate. The European Court tends to apply proportionality in a less searching manner. The Court does not wish to overburden itself with legal challenges. Furthermore, it may lack sufficient knowledge and expertise in a general policy to apply proportionality. However, if legislative measures are disproportionate, then the Court will invalidate them.

---

[20] See R. Barents, "The System of Deposits in Community Agricultural Law: Efficiency v Proportionality" (1985) 10 *EL Rev.* 239.

[21] Case 122/78 *SA Buitoni* v. *Fonds d'Orientation et de Régularisation des Marchés Agricoles* [1979] ECR 677.

[22] Case 181/84 *R.* v. *Intervention Board for Agricultural Produce (IBAP), ex parte E.D. & F. Man (Sugar) Ltd.* [1985] ECR 2885.

Whether the principle allows the Court to engage in a review of the merits has therefore been a central issue in the legitimacy of proportionality review. Some commentators have taken the view that since proportionality operates on a sliding scale of review it does not necessarily involve a substitution of the Court's view of the merits for that of the decision-maker.[23] However, this cannot be considered determinative. Arguing that the Court will only strike down measures that are *manifestly* disproportionate does not explain adequately whether this involves an illegitimate interference with the merits, or whether the Court is respecting the limits of its jurisdiction.

It may be questioned whether the focus on the issue of review of the merits is appropriate. The distinction between merits and legality can hardly be drawn in advance with any certainty. Instead, it may be more appropriate to inquire how proportionality contributes to achievement of chosen policy objectives. In this regard it is submitted that proportionality is used to optimise the interests of individuals to the extent that achievement of the policy goal remains factually possible. The Court does not examine the expediency of an administrative purpose, but considers whether it could have been satisfactorily obtained by a better-designed and less-onerous measure;[24] in other words, the Court undertakes a comparison of possible solutions to an administrative task. The tests of appropriateness and suitability determine whether the means chosen are capable of promoting the goal. As regards the necessity of a measure, it is clear that if there are no alternative means of achieving the objective it will be necessary to interfere with individual interests. By invalidating a measure as disproportionate the Court is, in effect, saying to the administrator: "we invalidate the decision you have made because we can think of a better decision—one that achieves your goals but at less cost to competing interests". The Court does not examine the expediency of attaining a certain objective, but questions the expediency of the means adopted to achieve that objective. This intricate inquiry of optimising competing values requires the Court to examine assessments of fact and appraise economic considerations.

It is submitted that review of the proportionality of a public measure is best understood within a purposive conception of administrative law. Law is used to advance policy goals and objectives as selected through the processes of political decision-making. The Court does not seek to impose its own set of values on what the administration ought to be doing. In finding the most effective means of protecting the individual the Court seeks to rationalise public action in light of the chosen policy objective. The identification of alternative possible courses of action is precisely the task with which an administrative jurisdiction ought to concern itself. Collective goals must be achieved and, if possible, through means which entail minimal interference with individual interests. Modern adminis-

---

[23] See, e.g., de Búrca, above at n. 4.

[24] See J. Temple Lang, "The Constitutional Principles Governing Community Legislation" (1989) 40 *NILQ* 227, 242; Lord Slynn, "European Law and the National Judge", in *Butterworth Lectures 1991–92* (Butterworths, London, 1993), 18, 28.

tration is simply too complex to suppose that the decision-maker will always take sufficient care in implementing policy. The role of the administrative court is to recognise what the administration wants to achieve and seek to accommodate individual interests as far as possible. To characterise proportionality as "the most potent weapon in the arsenal of the public law judge" is, mistaken.[25] This combative language obscures the role played by proportionality in promoting the achievement of policy objectives. As Francis Jacobs noted, proportionality is a "rational and well-structured test"[26] in which the courts "decide whether a particular exercise of power . . . [was] . . . the most appropriate way of achieving a particular policy goal".[27] Proportionality may be a far-reaching and intensive ground of review but it is precisely because the Court seeks to further the chosen policy goal that it avoids substitution of opinion.

PROPORTIONALITY IN ENGLISH LAW

Proportionality is "unknown" to English law.[28] English judges have no tradition of justifying their decisions by reference to the proportionality of public decision-making. The principle lacks an "authoritative presence" in the English legal tradition;[29] lawyers seeking to invoke it have been unable to draw upon any traditional authority in order to give an old phrase new content.[30] Furthermore, English lawyers consider that the notion of proportionality has a distinctly Continental sound to it. By contrast, reasonableness has a well-established common law lineage and is deeply entrenched in judicial discourse.[31] Following Lord Diplock's comment that proportionality might be adopted as a separate ground of review, there has been plenty of discussion over the merits and demerits of such a development.

While the debate tends to present proportionality as a transplant into the common law, it is not unknown for English judges to examine whether a penalty is disproportionate. For example, in the mid-seventeenth century the Court of King's Bench declared a fine imposed by the Commissioner of Sewers to be

---

[25] T. Tridimas, "Proportionality in Community Law: Searching for the Appropriate Standard of Scrutiny", in E. Ellis (ed.), *The Principle of Proportionality in the Laws of Europe* (Hart Publishing, Oxford, 1999), 65, 69.

[26] F.G. Jacobs, "Public Law—The Impact of Europe" [1999] *PL* 232, 239.

[27] F.G. Jacobs, "Recent Developments in the Principle of Proportionality in European Community Law", in Ellis (ed.), above at n. 25, 1, 20.

[28] J.F. Garner, "The Principle of Proportionality", in *UK National Reports Submitted to the Xth International Congress on Comparative Law* (Budapest, 1978), section IVD2/1.

[29] M. Krygier, "Law as Tradition" (1986) *5 Law and Philosophy* 237, 245–50.

[30] Cf. F.W. Maitland, "Why the History of English Law is not Written", in H.A.L. Fisher (ed.), *The Collected Papers of Frederic William Maitland Volume 1* (Cambridge University Press, Cambridge, 1911), 480, 491.

[31] See *Rooke's Case* (1598) 5 Co. Rep. 99b; *R. v. Askew* (1768) 4 Burr. 2186, 2189; *Kruse v. Johnson* [1898] 2 QB 91; *Theatre de Luxe (Halifax) Ltd. v. Gledhill* [1915] 2 KB 48, 58–60; *Associated Provincial Picture Houses Ltd. v. Wednesbury Corporation* [1948] 1 KB 223.

excessive and unreasonable.[32] Later that century, John Locke wrote that the law of nature allowed an individual to be punished only "so far as calm reason and conscience dictates, what is proportionate to his transgression, which is so much as may serve for reparation and restraint".[33] If, as Locke thought, the chief end of government was the preservation of property, then any penalty placed upon the enjoyment of such goods must be proportionate. However, the modern administrative state has experienced a huge expansion of the ends for which people engage in collective political organisation. How might proportionality be operationalised in this context? Should the courts impose their own view of the ends government ought to be pursuing or should they accept that the choice of ends remains a political decision and advise on the appropriate means to achieve those ends? The answer to these questions tends to turn upon a writer's own background assumptions concerning law and political thought. To understand the proportionality debate it is therefore necessary to appreciate the different conceptions of administrative law held by its contributors and, consequently, the different role proportionality plays within these conceptions.[34]

The proportionality debate

Those who adhere to what was described earlier as the traditional model of judicial review have rejected calls for the adoption of proportionality.[35] In this tradition the courts draw upon the artificial reason of the common law in order to protect individuals against unlawful administrative action. Underlying this model is an anti-rationalist approach to the role of law in government reflected in the adherence to the *Wednesbury* standard of review. When reviewing the exercise of discretionary powers judges should restrict themselves to asking whether the decision was "so unreasonable that no reasonable authority could ever have come to it".[36] Articulated by Lord Greene M.R., a judge with a formalistic approach to the judicial role,[37] and at a time when the judges were still in the throws of the wartime tendency of leaning "over backwards to the point of falling off the bench, in favour of the executive",[38] the *Wednesbury* standards have come to represent judicial restraint. However, at the same time, *Wednesbury* has allowed judicial intervention, even usurpation, but not on any principled or rational

---

[32]   *Commins v. Massam* (1643) March NR 196, 202. See L.L. Jaffe and E.G. Henderson, "Judicial Review and the Rule of Law" (1956) 72 *LQR* 345, 348–50, 355–7.

[33]   J. Locke, *Two Treatises of Government* [1689] (Everyman, London, 1993), II, § 8.

[34]   See, generally, M. Loughlin, *Public Law and Political Theory* (Clarendon Press, Oxford, 1992); *ibid.*, *Sword and Scales: An Examination of the Relationship between Law and Politics* (Hart Publishing, Oxford, 2000).

[35]   See ch. 1 above.

[36]   *Wednesbury*, above at n. 31, 230.

[37]   See Lord Greene, *The Judicial Office* (The Holdsworth Society, Birmingham, 1938); Lord Greene, "Law and Progress" (1944) 94 *The Law Journal* 349, 357, 365.

[38]   J.A.G. Griffith, *Administrative Law and the Judges* (The Pritt Memorial Lecture, London, 1978), 13.

basis.[39] *Wednesbury* is therefore a rule of artificial reason used to avoid policy questions, but which simultaneously affords the judges sufficient discretion to express their (dis-)approval of public decisions. As Sir Stephen Sedley succinctly observed, *Wednesbury* "invented nothing and clarified little".[40]

As a result of changes in government and dissatisfaction with the limits placed on judicial review by the traditional model, some writers have sought to develop a more rational model of judicial review premised upon liberal constitutionalism.[41] Within this modernised liberal approach, law is viewed as deriving from principles, not rules. Judges articulate points of principle but not policy.[42] Liberal constitutionalists have been attracted to proportionality since they see it as a rational principle that can be used to protect individual freedom. They essentially want to replace the formal Diceyan conception of the rule of law with a more substantive conception in order to uphold individual freedom against the state. The issue of whether English law should embrace proportionality has become a central issue between the traditional and liberal conceptions of judicial review. What is important to note here is that both approaches adopt a normative orientation. Law is viewed as separate from the purposes of governance. Whereas in the traditional approach the conventional wisdom of the common law supplies this normative quality, liberals consider that rational principles are required to protect constitutional liberty.

The foremost advocates of proportionality have been Jeffrey Jowell and Anthony Lester, who have sought to extend the approach of Lord Diplock in the rationalisation of the heads of judicial review.[43] Their argument is that *Wednesbury* unreasonableness is a deficient articulation of substantive review and that principles such as proportionality are required to provide more principled justification for judicial intervention and to protect individual rights. Judges require a more principled method of upholding the rule of law than the inadequate and tautologous *Wednesbury* test. Accordingly, Jowell and Lester argue that the requirement that the means should bear a proportionate relationship with the desired end seems so "characteristically English" that there should be little difficulty in absorbing this principle into English law.[44] They also claim that implicit applications of the principle can be found "lurking

---

[39] See, e.g., *Wheeler* v. *Leicester City Council* [1985] AC 1054.

[40] S. Sedley, "Governments, Constitutions and Judges", in G. Richardson and H. Genn (eds), *Administrative Law and Government Action: The Courts and Alternative Mechanisms of Review* (Clarendon Press, Oxford, 1994), 35, 38.

[41] See, e.g., T.R.S. Allan, *Law, Liberty, and Justice: The Foundations of British Constitutionalism* (Clarendon Press, Oxford, 1993).

[42] Cf. R. Dworkin, *Taking Rights Seriously* (Duckworth, London, 1977); *ibid.*, *Law's Empire* (Fontana, London, 1986).

[43] J. Jowell and A. Lester, "Beyond *Wednesbury*: Substantive Principles of Administrative Law" [1987] *PL* 368; J. Jowell and A. Lester, "Proportionality: Neither Novel Nor Dangerous", in J. Jowell and D. Oliver (eds), *New Directions in Judicial Review* (Stevens, London, 1988), 51; J. Jowell, "Is Proportionality an Alien Concept?" (1996) 2 *EPL* 401.

[44] Jowell and Lester, "Beyond *Wednesbury*: Substantive Principles of Administrative Law", above at n. 43, 375.

within the underbrush of *Wednesbury*".[45] Judges have applied notions of proportionality without knowing it, or more likely, without admitting it. In the absence of any traditional authority advocates of proportionality have resorted to interpreting previous case law in light of this principle to support their argument.[46] The recognition that proportionality appears too Continental for English judges to recognise as a discrete category of review has recently been made by Jowell, who stated that "[p]roportionality is perhaps . . . *unreasonableness* under a different name, but it is a more pointed principle".[47] At one level the argument could be viewed as an invitation for the judiciary to change their language of review. However, Jowell and Lester envisage a more principled and coherent form of review rather than the traditional focus on remedies. Judicial acceptance of proportionality is viewed as the means to achieve this.

This argument has received significant support from the extra-judicial publications of Sir John Laws who, in 1993, sought to demonstrate that despite the lack of any explicit protection of fundamental rights in the British Constitution, the common law could remedy this deficiency.[48] In his article, Laws argued that in order to protect fundamental rights a differential standard of judicial protection should be developed which varies depending on the impact of public power upon the individual. The greater the intrusion by a public body over the citizen into an area concerning fundamental rights the more compelling justification must be demonstrated. For Laws, the "monolithic" standard of irrationality is "an imperfect and inappropriate mechanism for the development of differential standards in judicial review".[49] When a public authority takes a decision affecting an individual's fundamental rights it should accord priority to the affected right unless it can, to the court's satisfaction, provide substantial justification for overriding it:[50]

> "if we are to entertain a form of review in which fundamental rights are to enjoy the court's distinct protection, the very exercise consists in *an insistence that the decision-maker is not free to order his priorities as he chooses* . . . If a government or a local authority, *perhaps too much in love with a particular policy objective*, were to take a decision which curtails free speech for *no convincing reason*, to excoriate it as having lost its sense looks a little too much like sending people with *unacceptable politics* to the psychiatric hospital. The deployment of proportionality sets in focus the *true nature* of the exercise: the elaboration of *a rule about permissible priorities*."

---

[45] Ibid., 374. See also M. Hunt, *Using Human Rights Law in English Courts* (Hart Publishing, Oxford, 1997), 216.

[46] For criticism, see S. Boyron, "Proportionality in English Administrative Law: A Faulty Translation?"(1992) 12 *OJLS* 237.

[47] J. Jowell, "Restraining the State: Politics, Principle and Judicial Review" (1997) 50 *CLP* 189, 209 (special edition entitled *Law and Opinion at the End of the Twentieth Century*).

[48] J. Laws, "Is the High Court the Guardian of Fundamental Constitutional Rights?" [1993] *PL* 59.

[49] Ibid., 69.

[50] Ibid., 73–4 (emphasis added).

Laws considered that proportionality is constructed as a rule of permissible priorities rather than an examination of permissible courses of action to be tested in a goal-oriented balancing exercise. By adopting such a conception it appears fully open to the court to moralise over what objectives the public authority should or should not pursue, rather than examine the various courses of action to find a more suitable and less-restrictive means of implementing a policy objective. Similarly, Jowell, in discussing proportionality, commented:[51]

> "It is . . . one of the hallmarks of tyranny that means may be sacrificed to ends. And a hallmark of liberty that fidelity to the ends of public policy should not inevitably justify the means of attaining it."

For liberal constitutionalists then, proportionality is a means of "restraining the state" and determining the "proper limits of governmental power".[52]

The conception of proportionality adopted by Laws and Jowell is very different from its sense in European Community law because it overlooks the role of the court in examining the viability of alternative courses of action for achieving the desired objective. In some cases there may be no alternative means available to the public authority. However, if the court nevertheless declares the measure to be disproportionate, it will have, in effect, prevented the public authority from pursuing its legitimate objective. In other words, if fidelity to the ends of public policy does not always justify the means of attaining it, this implies that the court has room to prevent the achievement of the public goal by refusing to ensure that alternative means are available. As we have seen above, in European Community law it is clear that if a less-restrictive, alternative course of action is not available, it is necessary to interfere with private interests. Merely to state that the means adopted are disproportionate is insufficient; the European Court will suggest an alternative course of action that is equally capable of achieving the desired end. However, liberal constitutionalists such as Laws and Jowell consider that the purposive element of the principle is de-emphasised. Instead, proportionality has become an integral principle within a liberal framework of law in which the judge can review the ends of public action. This is a radical transformation of the meaning of proportionality. The principle has effectively been re-conceptualised from a means of promoting policy objectives to a means of detailing the permissible priorities of public action.

The central issue here is the relationship between law and government. For Sir John Laws proportionality is a "principle of a free society" and therefore "logically prior to the policies of elected government".[53] This is at variance with the more purposive approach of European Community law. It is clear the liberal argument uses proportionality for a purpose other than seeking to incorporate

---

[51] Jowell, above at n. 47, 209.

[52] Ibid., 190. See also J. Jowell, "Of Vires and Vacuums: The Constitutional Context of Judicial Review" [1999] *PL* 448.

[53] J. Laws, "*Wednesbury*", in C. Forsyth and I. Hare (eds), *The Golden Metwand and the Crooked Cord: Essays on Public Law in Honour of Sir William Wade QC* (Clarendon Press, Oxford, 1998), 185, 201.

European concepts in light of the impact of European law. Liberal constitutionalists view the principle as a means of instituting an idealised conception of the
relationship between the individual and the state premised upon liberal values.
Consequently, the principle is injected with some normative content on the
nature of "a free society" and the "proper reach of governmental activity" which
is supplied by theories of political liberalism or, for Sir John Laws, by Kant's
categorical imperative that individuals are always to be treated as an end in
themselves and never as a means only.[54] Even Paul Craig, who has provided a
constructive and thoughtful argument advocating the use of proportionality in
English law,[55] has stated that the principle requires some choice between competing political philosophies, such as utilitarianism or Rawlsian liberalism.[56] If
so, this involves the court adopting some political conception of the competing
interests which uses proportionality as a means of limiting state activity.
Liberals have constructed an *a priori* conception of law in which proportionality is used under the banner of "fundamental moral principles" to judge the purpose for which the public authority acts.[57] Purposive rationality has been
supplanted by liberal rationalism within an entirely different conception of
administrative law. The functional analysis of the European Court is replaced
by the moralising of the philosopher-judge Hercules.[58]

The response to the liberal case in favour of proportionality has been made
by those seeking to maintain the traditional conception of judicial review. Lord
Irvine, for example, has reaffirmed the need for observance of the "constitutional imperative of judicial self-restraint", as exemplified in the *Wednesbury*
principles.[59] As proportionality exceeds these time-honoured limits it should be
rejected as incompatible with the traditions of English law. Irvine considers that
proportionality "invites review of the merits of public decisions . . . and would
involve the court in a process of policy evaluation which goes far beyond its
allotted constitutional role".[60] Proportionality is viewed as a "novel and dangerous" principle which the courts should refuse to entertain.[61]

Irvine's argument is essentially drawn from the approach of the House of
Lords in *Brind*,[62] in particular the speeches of Lords Ackner and Lowry, and
therefore implicitly adopts the same misconceptions which infused the robust

---

[54] Ibid. See also J. Laws, "The Constitution: Morals and Rights" [1996] *PL* 622.

[55] P.P. Craig, "Proportionality: Lessons from Community Law", *The European Advocate*
(Spring 1994), 2; P.P. Craig, "Unreasonableness and Proportionality in UK Law", in Ellis (ed.),
above at n. 25, 85.

[56] P.P. Craig, *Administrative Law* (Sweet & Maxwell, London, 4th ed. 1999), 606.

[57] J. Laws, "The Constitutional Foundations of Modern Public Law" (1998) 10 *European Review
of Public Law* 579, 586. On the ambiguity of "fundamental laws", see C. Hill, *The Century of
Revolution 1603–1714* (Routledge, London, 2nd ed. 1980), 55.

[58] Cf. Dworkin, above at n. 42.

[59] Lord Irvine of Lairg Q.C., "Judges and Decision-Makers: The Theory and Practice of
Wednesbury Review" [1996] *PL* 59, 60.

[60] Ibid., 74.

[61] *Allied Dunbar (Frank Weisinger) Ltd.* v. *Frank Weisinger* [1988] 17 IRLR 60, 65, *per* Millett J.

[62] *R.* v. *Secretary of State for the Home Department, ex parte Brind* [1991] 1 AC 696.

denunciation of proportionality made there. In rejecting the invitation to use proportionality to review the restriction placed on the broadcasting of words spoken by representatives of terrorist organisations, Lords Ackner and Lowry sought further to ensure that the principle would not gain any future recognition in English law.[63] However, this refusal to recognise proportionality appears to have been based on a misunderstanding of the principle, as demonstrated in Lord Ackner's opinion. The following formulation had been advanced in argument: "could the minister reasonably conclude that his direction was necessary?".[64] Since the proportionality test is a way of matching up the appropriate means to achieve the desired policy objective, it might be thought that this formulation should have been understood as an invitation for the court to ask whether an alternative, less-restrictive course of action was available. However, in Lord Ackner's opinion this test did not mean that the court should examine whether alternative courses equally effective in achieving the minister's objective were available. Rather, it required a balancing of "the reasons, pro and con, for . . . [the] . . . decision".[65] In other words, Lord Ackner confused the proportionality test with an examination of the very reasons for the policy. The judges were unable to appreciate that proportionality was not an invitation for the court to substitute its own opinion of the aim behind the measure for that of the decision-maker, but a way of rationalising the achievement of that aim. Owing to their ignorance of a developed doctrine of Community law, Lords Ackner and Lowry refused to recognise the existence of proportionality in English law. While *Brind* has been celebrated as "the high water mark of the courts' strict adherence to the *Wednesbury* principles",[66] this out-of-hand rejection of proportionality was essentially predicated on a mistaken understanding of the doctrine.

A more developed argument has been advanced by Lord Hoffmann,[67] whose case against proportionality derives from the distinctive nature of the common law of judicial review. Rather than being an area of law capable of rendering precise rules, "the whole art of judicial review . . . requires a political sensitivity to the proper boundaries between the powers of the legislative, executive and judicial branches of government".[68] The subtle and complex process of judicial review cannot be reduced to mere labels but must recognise the practical experience of the judges. As "[t]here are no hard and fast rules to tell judges how . . . [to reconcile democratic government and fundamental rights] . . . they have

---

[63] According to Lord Hoffmann,"Lord Lowry's attitude to proportionality was rather like that of the Caliph of Baghdad to the books in the library of Alexandria: either they said the same as the Koran and should be burned as superfluous or they said something different and should be burned as heretical": "A Sense of Proportion" (1997) 32 *Irish Jurist* 49, 59.

[64] *Brind*, above at n. 62, 762G, 766F.

[65] Ibid., 762H.

[66] Irvine, above at n. 59, 74.

[67] Lord Hoffmann, above at n. 63; Lord Hoffmann, "The Influence of the European Principle of Proportionality upon UK Law", in Ellis (ed.), above at n. 25, 107.

[68] Ibid., 110.

to tread a delicate line which avoids the extremes of populism on the one hand and judicial over-activism on the other".[69] Here we can see the emphasis upon law as a form of practical, as opposed to technical, knowledge which is not susceptible of precise formulation. In articulating their artificial reason, the courts have to use their political experience to maintain the delicate constitutional balance. The assumption is that law does not identify the legitimate objectives of the public interest and seek to promote them; it is a separate phenomenon rooted in the practical experience of the judges.

Working from this conception, Lord Hoffmann views the practice of assigning cases to particular sub-species of proportionality, which afflicts German administrative law, as a distraction from the real issue. English law avoids such technical classification because it has a general principle of unreasonableness. The important issue, according to Lord Hoffmann, is who should decide whether this principle has been observed. Should the court accept the public authority's decision, or should it impose its own view of the matter? The comparison involved between the social importance of the objective to be achieved and the burdens imposed by the means used to achieve it is a matter of social and economic judgment to be entrusted to Parliament. While judges will strike down a decision if it is unreasonable, they use their political sensitivity in drawing the boundary of decision-making. When compared with the all-important question of the appropriate margin of appreciation to be afforded to decision-making, the task of assigning cases to the various categories of proportionality is "no better than train spotting".[70] Lord Hoffmann's case against proportionality is essentially an argument to maintain faith in the conventional wisdom of the judges. For Lord Hoffmann the customary wisdom of the courts as articulated through the language of reasonableness cannot, except in a very crude manner, be expressed through the technical rules of proportionality. The error of proportionality is to attempt to reduce this accummulated experience to precise rules and, thereby, devalue it.

Through Lord Hoffmann's views on the judges as the expositors of their political experience rather than as organs of the state, we can gain an insight into his views on the role of law in government. The purpose of law is to control and check administration rather than contribute towards the achievement of its objectives. Law should not seek an optimal balance between the realisation of social goals and the protection of individual interests, but correct decisions only when they exceed certain unspecifiable limits. It is precisely this difference in orientation that, it is submitted, underlies English and European administrative law. However, Lord Hoffmann would appear not to accept this

---

[69] Ibid.

[70] Ibid., 113. At p. 109 Lord Hoffmann comments that "[t]o go down the road of classification can lead only to metaphysical problems of distinguishing different forms or irrationality which would truly be worthy of mediaeval schoolmen and, if such distinctions are to have any practical meaning, difference in the treatment of different kinds of irrationality which could fairly be characterised as irrational".

since he has stated that the courts in England, Europe and Germany engage in the resolution of the same problems by substantially the same methods:[71]

> "Whether the courts ride into battle with proportionality or rationality inscribed on their banners, the weapons they carry to defend the citizen against the State are much the same."

However, as indicated earlier, the metaphorical battle between judges and the administration is an inappropriate way of understanding proportionality review.[72] The idea that the administrative court uses proportionality as a weapon to gain an advantage over the administration simply epitomises the problematic nature of the debate. As the basic orientation underpinning common law has failed to respond constructively to the growth in scale and complexity of state activity, law has come to be seen as a means of preventing "the powerful engines of authority . . . from running amok".[73] Unlike the Continental tradition, law is not viewed as a means of structuring or guiding administrative action in the pursuit of collective goals. This difference in orientation towards the role of law in administration affects perceptions towards concepts such as proportionality. English lawyers approach proportionality from the view that law is about identifying the limits of public action rather than an integral feature in the achievement of such tasks. The central function of proportionality of rationalising the impact of public decisions to the extent that the public interest remains achievable is therefore overlooked. A misunderstanding of this nature demonstrates the dangers of comparing concepts without situating them within the wider context of the cultural orientation towards the role of law in government.

Given the strength of the European tide, Lord Hoffmann may be viewed as acting out the role of a Canute. Not even he can prevent applicants from exercising their full rights under European law.[74] However, at the same time his views clearly identify the divergent approach to law and administration. Judicial review in Europe is not seen as a form of judicial art reliant upon the judiciary's political sensitivity and artificial reason. The limited patterns of thought in English administrative law, reflected in the dualisms of judicial activism and restraint, legality and merits, appear to be incapable of adequately accommodating the full meaning of proportionality.

From a different perspective, Carol Harlow has also cautioned against the adoption of proportionality. Starting from the premise that law is essentially a form of political activity, Harlow's empirical and positivist style of functionalism is highly sceptical of any extension of judicial review.[75] Harlow considers

---

[71] Lord Hoffmann, above at n. 63, 60.

[72] See p. 85 above.

[73] H.W.R. Wade and C.F. Forsyth, *Administrative Law* (Clarendon Press, Oxford, 7th ed. 1994), 5.

[74] See *Stoke-on-Trent City Council* v. *B & Q plc* [1991] Ch. 48 (Hoffman J.). See p. 106 below.

[75] See J.A.G. Griffith, "The Political Constitution" (1979) 42 *MLR* 1; J.A.G. Griffith, "Constitutional and Administrative Law", in P. Archer and A. Martin (eds), *More Law Reform Now: A Collection of Essays on Law Reform* (Barry Rose, Chichester, 1983), 49, 54–9.

that the claims made over the precision and rationality of civil law are exaggerated and arguments in favour of proportionality show little awareness of the principle as a "'balancing test' replete with judicial discretion".[76] Under the "green light" theory, which views the development of administrative action as a sign of social progress,[77] the matters involved in a proportionality inquiry are too important to be left solely to judges.[78] From this perspective, proportionality would enable the judges to replace administrative discretion with judicial discretion and should be rejected as a potential restriction of democratic government: "law is not and cannot be a substitute for politics".[79] This argument certainly has strength when set against the conception of proportionality advanced by the liberals—the role they envisage for proportionality clearly involves the courts preventing public authorities from pursuing certain goals if they do not conform to certain liberal assumptions concerning the proper relationship between individuals and the state. If the principle is to be used as a way of "blocking a course of action entirely on the ground that it is a disproportionate method of attaining the legislator's objectives" without ensuring that an equally effective course is available, the criticism that law is interfering in politics without justification is difficult to rebut.[80]

However, if the principle is utilised within a purposive and rational conception of administrative law, it becomes less clear that law should always defer to the political process. Since the administrator may fail adequately to accommodate affected interests, there is a need for a jurisdiction to operate in this area of law and administration. In applying proportionality the administrative court invalidates a decision only when an alternative course of action was available which was equally effective for the achievement of the selected goal. As such, can proportionality review be accused of restricting democratic government? It is submitted that if adjudication is oriented towards the furtherance of goals selected through the processes of political decision-making, then it can improve the quality of governance. Furthermore, it is questionable whether the empirical conception of law provides an appropriate framework in which to situate proportionality. If the principle is used to rationalise public decisions in light of their objective, it is difficult to view law as a possible substitute for politics. Instead, it would be more appropriate to view law as responsive to the social function selected through the processes of political decision-making.

---

[76] C. Harlow, "Changing the Mindset: The Place of Theory in English Administrative Law" (1994) 14 *OJLS* 419, 428–9.

[77] See C. Harlow and R. Rawlings, *Law and Administration* (Butterworths, London, 2nd ed. 1998), ch. 3.

[78] C. Harlow, "Back to Basics: Reinventing Administrative Law" [1997] *PL* 245, 261.

[79] Griffith (1979), above at n. 75, 16.

[80] Harlow and Rawlings, above at n. 77, 118. For a critical assessment of the views of Sir John Laws from this perspective see J.A.G. Griffith, "The Brave New World of Sir John Laws" (2000) 63 *MLR* 159.

Assessing the debate

It has been contended that to understand the discussion concerning proportionality it is necessary to look behind the arguments presented and situate them within the different styles of public law thought. The case for proportionality has, in large part, been made by public lawyers seeking to institute a liberal conception of law, the individual and the state. On this view, proportionality is a principle of liberal morality which identifies the necessary limits of governmental power. The purpose of proportionality as a constitutional principle is the protection of the individual against the state. The response to such arguments has typically been made by those in high judicial office and therefore deeply rooted in the common law tradition. Their dislike of proportionality is that it involves the courts in policy matters. However, this argument should be interpreted from the tradition from which it derives. In deciding cases, common law judges draw on accumulated wisdom and practical experience to articulate certain values. The common law is not a legal science capable of being defined in clear and precise rules but, as Lord Hoffmann explains, is more a form of art. Given this cultural orientation, judges have been extremely reluctant to give up their customary doctrines for a Continental principle which requires coherent and explicit rationalisation. Judges implicitly accept that they cannot avoid policy issues, but prefer to handle such questions in their customary manner, thereby maintaining the fiction of the separation of powers.

The proportionality debate has largely been conducted between adherents of these two styles of thought. Liberals have eagerly advocated proportionality in order to interpret the law in light of their own background theory of political liberalism. Traditionalists, such as Lord Irvine, have urged caution and restraint in favour of conventional common law doctrines. In this context proportionality has acted as a "legal irritant" and has "infected the interplay of discourses" concerning the proper reach of judicial review in England.[81] Once introduced into this different cultural context, the meaning of proportionality has been reconstructed to suit the needs of the domestic debate. Liberals have been attracted to the more rational and structured nature of proportionality, but have ignored its purposive role. Instead, they have sought to situate the principle within a liberal conception of the relationship between the individual and the state. In response to this new form of discourse the internal context has experienced an important change. Traditionalists have sought to reaffirm the need for "*Wednesbury* review".[82] The disorientation in this style of thought has given rise to an ideological re-traditionalisation of customary wisdom. The call

[81] G. Teubner, "Legal Irritants: Good Faith in British Law or How Unifying Law Ends Up in New Divergences" (1998) 61 *MLR* 11, 12.
[82] Irvine, above at n. 59. See also Sir Robert Carnwath, "The Reasonable Limits of Local Authority Powers" [1996] *PL* 244.

for *Wednesbury* limits to be strictly observed should be interpreted as an ideological response to such strain.[83]

The debate has not generally recognised that proportionality has developed within a different conception of administrative law. For example, much discussion has been spent analysing whether there is any conceptual difference between unreasonableness and proportionality without acknowledging that these concepts serve different purposes within entirely different conceptions of administrative law.[84] This has ignored the contrast between an English judge, using his conventional wisdom to decide whether the exercise of a non-purposively defined discretionary power was unreasonable or irrational,[85] and the European Court, determining in light of the objective of a regulation whether alternative courses of action were available and which were equally capable of promoting the desired end. The difference is between an administrative jurisdiction seeking to ensure the sensitive treatment of individuals compatible with the achievement of collective goals, and a High Court judge tempted to interfere with a decision because it offends his own sense of right or wrong.

While the debate has been conducted between the traditional and liberal perspectives, neither seems capable of adequately integrating the notion of proportionality as it is understood in European law. The idea that law can facilitate policy objectives as well as rationalise their impact on individuals has been completely overlooked. In modern societies governance is a highly complex activity. It is impossible to expect that the limited political experience of the judiciary can provide any rational guidance to the achievement of administrative tasks. The cultural orientation underlying *Wednesbury* review is no longer adequate because it has been surpassed by social change as reflected in the development of modern governance. The traditionalist conception of law has failed to provide a constructive response to the positivisation of law for the achievement of social purposes. Liberals recognise the inadequacies of conventional wisdom and seek to rationalise the common law through the elucidation of principle. However, their project seeks to place the relationship between the state and the individual within an idealised framework. This mode of thought rests upon certain value assumptions concerning the "proper limits of governmental

---

[83] Cf. C. Geertz, "Ideology as a Cultural System", in *The Interpretation of Cultures* (Fontana, London, 1993), 193, 219.

[84] See, e.g., Lord Mackenzie Stuart, "Control of Power Within the European Communities" (1986) 11 *Holdsworth LR* 1, 13; D. Wyatt, "European Community Law and Public Law in the United Kingdom", in B.S. Markesinis (ed.), *The Gradual Convergence: Foreign ideas, Foreign Influences and English Law on the Eve of the 21st Century* (Clarendon Press, Oxford, 1994), 188, 195–8; G. de Búrca, "Proportionality and *Wednesbury* Unreasonableness: The Influence of Legal Concepts on UK Law" (1997) 3 *EPL* 561; D. Oulton, "How Widely Accepted as a General Principle is Proportionality?" (1997) 12 *Commonwealth Judicial Journal* 17.

[85] Alternatively, in *R. v. Devon County Council, ex parte G* [1989] AC 573, 577G, 583H, Lord Donaldson M.R. questioned the definition of irrationality as "casting doubt on the mental capacity of the decision-maker". His Lordship preferred the test of whether the decision could elicit the response "my goodness, that is certainly wrong".

power".[86] Sir John Laws is correct to state that there is "something of a mis-match between the use of . . . [proportionality] . . . in Europe and the buffers against which it has run in England".[87] However, it cannot be assumed that liberal constitutionalism provides an adequate framework in which to integrate proportionality. The tendency of this style of thought is to use law to review the ends of public action rather than advise on the appropriate means of pursuing legitimate objectives as selected through political decision-making processes.

Furthermore, the liberal constitutionalists tend to adopt a "citizen versus the state" approach to public law and urge the use of proportionality to restrain government. However, proportionality has been developed against the assumption that modern administration is essential to individual well-being because it serves certain social purposes. As Advocate-General Trabucchi noted, "the fulfilment of tasks incumbent on the State may call for adjustments in the degree of freedom which the subjective right of the individual represents".[88] It is as much in the interests of the individual that the administration can achieve its objectives effectively as it is in the state's interests that it can complete its tasks with the co-operation of the individual.

The justification of proportionality therefore is that it provides a method of achieving an optimal balance between the securing of collective goals and the protection of individual interests. Proportionality does not detract from the fulfilment of public goals but insists that public authorities pay sufficient regard to the interests of individuals in resolving on the methods of attaining their objectives. Protection of the individual is an issue only as long as the public objective is capable of being achieved.

CONCLUSION

In this chapter it has been argued that the debate concerning proportionality can best be understood when set against the different approaches to administrative law. Arguments concerning the doctrine reflect different ideas of what courts should be doing in judicial review proceedings. To say that courts should strive to uphold the standards of legality merely begs the question of which specific conception of legality should be upheld. While proportionality has been the subject of extensive debate among English lawyers, they have nevertheless failed to elucidate how English courts might operate a review similar to that of the European Court. Essentially, the debate has overlooked the fact that proportionality in European law is predicated upon the assumption that law should contribute to the purposive rationality of administrative decision-making.

---

[86] Jowell, above at n. 47.

[87] J. Laws, "English and Community Law: Uniformity of Principle", *The European Advocate* (Autumn, 1994), 2, 4.

[88] Case 118/75 *Criminal Proceedings against Watson and Belmann* [1975] ECR 1185, 1209 (col. 1) of the Advocate-General's opinion.

Despite its foreignness, misunderstandings over its meaning and the refusal of English judges to acknowledge it, proportionality continues to present a distinctive challenge for the common law. Understanding the nature of the discussion so far is the first step. The next step is to identify how English law can prepare the way ahead for the effective application of the principle. A clearer elucidation of this thesis is provided in the next chapter.

5

Proportionality (II): Future Development

E VER SINCE LORD Diplock first advanced the possibility that proportionality might be available as a separate head of judicial review, its precise status has been uncertain. However, over the last few years a number of factors have coalesced, making the formal recognition of proportionality highly likely. First, the increasing impact of European Community law requires public administrators and the courts to give full effect to Community rights and obligations. This impact is educating administrators and judges by requiring them to deal with the types of issues involved in applying proportionality. It is also providing a platform on which a self-critique of the adequacy of national practices may be undertaken. Among all the judicial soul-searching, it is being recognised gradually that proportionality provides a more structured and coherent tool to examine public decisions by a judiciary willing to undertake a more intensive review. Unreasonableness is a useful formula on which an application for review may be rejected, but it may promote claims of political bias when used to strike down a decision. Proportionality may be used to rebut such claims because it enables courts to minimise the impact of public decisions on individuals by advising on alternative means of achieving public authorities' objectives.

Secondly, if courts continue to draw a strict division between the standards employed in judicial review under European Community law and domestic law, then the standard of English law may be viewed as second class in the sense that it is not as rigorous and comprehensive as that undertaken by the European Court of Justice. Finally, the Human Rights Act 1998 was passed in order to give further effect to the rights and liberties guaranteed under the European Convention of Human Rights. In order to measure public decision-making against the standards set down in the Convention and developed by the European Court of Human Rights, English courts will need to employ proportionality.

The cumulative effect of these factors is that English judges can no longer reject proportionality out of hand. One way or another they will be required to undertake the type of assessments involved in a proportionality inquiry. In light of this it would be instructive to inquire how, in practical terms, a principle predicated on purposive rationality could be integrated into English law. The argument advanced here is that if English judges are to integrate this principle, it would require more than just a change of language; judges would also have to re-orient the role and purpose of judicial review.

A court applying proportionality must possess two essential requirements. First, the court must know of the objective(s) served by the measure. Secondly, the court must have the ability to assess whether it was factually possible for the public authority to have used alternative measures which were equally effective for the achievement of the objective. These two aspects of proportionality will be considered in the first two sections of this chapter. The third section will consider how, in practice, judicial review of the proportionality of public decision-making will work.

1. PROPORTIONALITY AND PUBLIC OBJECTIVES

In examining the proportionality of a public measure the court is asking whether a better measure could have been adopted to achieve the same goal. The court therefore needs to be informed of the purposes of public action. If the court does not know which purposes are being pursued by the measure, or if those purposes are vague and obscure, it will be unable to determine whether the same policy result could satisfactorily have been secured by another course of action. In this regard English courts appear to be under a distinct disadvantage when compared with the European Court of Justice and Continental courts. In the United Kingdom the ends of state action are not usually specified, whereas on the other side of the English Channel and in the European Community generally there tends to be a strong tradition of legalism and a concern for the formalisation of political power reflected in the explicit identification of purposes in law-making.

For example, in the Federal Republic of Germany, where administrative courts scrutinise the proportionality of public action closely, the objectives served by legislation and administrative decisions are clearly expressed. The German Basic Law states that the Government may be authorised by a law to issue ordinances; the content, purpose and scope of powers conferred by such ordinances must be set forth in the law.[1] Similarly, the EC Treaty requires that regulations, directives and decisions state the reasons on which they are based.[2] In Britain, by comparison, there is no similar constitutional requirement for delegated legislation to specify the purposes for which it was adopted. Whether such law-making refers to the reasons for which it was adopted or the objectives it is designed to achieve tends to depend on specific requirements in legislation or established practice.

This difference may be said to reflect a wider divergence between the constitutions of the United Kingdom, on the one hand, and those of Continental

---

[1] Article 80(1) of the German Basic Law.
[2] Article 253 of the EC Treaty.

Europe and the European Community, on the other. The former is informal and practical, whereas the latter tend to be more rational and formalised. The British constitution is an unwritten tradition based on precedent and convention, which is imparted and handed down to successive generations through the practical knowledge of its participants. It is a "tradition of behaviour . . . [which] . . . is neither fixed nor finished; it has no changeless centre to which understanding can anchor itself; there is no sovereign purpose to be perceived or invariable direction to be detected". Since everything in this tradition is temporary, its identity is a principle of continuity through which "authority is diffused between past, present and future".[3]

By contrast, Continental constitutions tend to exhibit a more rational and formalised orientation. The constitution guides political action by positively requiring public authorities to achieve formulated purposes. The EC Treaty, for example, begins by specifying the tasks and activities of the Community and the purposes assigned to it. The Treaty also details the role and powers of European institutions, which must adopt appropriate measures for the attainment of those objectives.

The application of proportionality would therefore appear to be particularly suited to the more formalised Continental approach, rather than the informal and pragmatic British tradition. Only by knowing the purposes of public action are courts able to examine whether other measures could instead have been adopted. As the British constitution does not contain any formulated list of purposes to which political activity is directed towards, review of the proportionality of public measures could easily collapse into a review of the merits. Members of the judiciary have, on occasion, made intimations towards this point. In 1959 Lord Parker remarked that "in modern Britain, where no agreement exists on the ends of Society and the means of achieving those ends, it would be disastrous if the courts did not eschew the temptation to pass judgment on an issue of policy". Consequently, "[j]udicial self-preservation may . . . alone dictate restraint".[4]

It could be argued that as a result of the different constitutional frameworks, proportionality can have little role in English law. However, the difference may be more apparent than real. Mitchell's comment that British "constitutional law is formed for us as a result of the activities of men and institutions working towards ends which are often only broadly conceived and only partly defined or,

---

[3] M. Oakeshott, *Rationalism in Politics* (Methuen, London, 1962), 128. It may be noted that British constitutional thought has, at times, emphasised the need to structure government around agreed ends. For example, Tom Paine, in *Rights of Man* [1791] (Penguin, Harmondsworth, 1984), 198, remarked that "[i]n forming a constitution, it is first necessary to consider what are the ends for which government is necessary? Secondly, what are the best means, and the least expensive, for accomplishing those ends?" Paine was, of course, responding to Edmund Burke, who praised the inheritable nature of the constitution because it demonstrated "the happy effect of following nature, which is wisdom without reflection": *Reflections on the Revolution in France* [1790] (Penguin, Harmondsworth, 1982), 119.

[4] Lord Parker of Waddington, *Recent Developments in the Supervisory Powers of the Courts Over Inferior Tribunals* (Magnes Press, Jerusalem, 1959), 27–8.

indeed, understood by the actors" could not be made in such an unqualified fashion today.[5] In common with other European states, government in the United Kingdom has taken on responsibility for the management of the economy and the social welfare of its citizens. The state intervenes in the social sphere in order to achieve a multiplicity of public purposes. It regulates markets and ensures free competition. It makes provision for health and education, regulates the transport system and protects the environment. As in other countries, the state provides a public sphere in which social issues are debated and problems are resolved by resort to collective action. However, in Britain we have been unable to construct a more modernised understanding of the constitution that suits contemporary conditions of social complexity. Unlike other states and the European Community, rather than develop a legal concept of the state as the body through which collective action is organised, British public law has preferred to retain the dignified symbol of the Crown to explain legislative and executive law-making.

With the growth of state activities, a more basic change has occurred in the role of law. Law has become an instrument of social change used by political authorities to achieve their policy goals. As Niklas Luhmann has explained, the validity of modern law is "now based upon its function. This validity is interpreted in light of the future".[6] Modern positive law, in the form of rules, regulations and statutory instruments, is valid by reason of a political decision concerning social development. In the English legal system, these insights have rarely been acknowledged. Instead, law tends to be viewed as a respository of moral values. But this conception of law is no longer an adequate framework in which to integrate proportionality. That principle concerns the effective implementation of public policy. In assessing proportionality of a measure, courts must focus upon the specific objective that the political authority wanted to realise. In summary, the functional basis of modern law needs to be accepted if proportionality is to be utilised.

If we turn to the application of proportionality, what difficulties can the English courts expect to face? The main difficulty would appear to derive from the reluctance of Parliament to detail the purposes pursued by legislation in a preamble. If, for example, administrative powers are conferred by legislation for the purpose of obtaining a specified policy result, this contributes to the court's task of ensuring proportionality in public decision-making. In light of the specified objective, the court can assess whether the public authority could have utilised an alternative course of action. According to Lord Mackenzie Stuart, a former judge at the European Court, the importance of preambles in Community legislation cannot be over-emphasised; they facilitate the court's task of reviewing legality.[7]

---

[5] J.D.B. Mitchell, *Constitutional Law* (Green, Edinburgh, 2nd ed. 1968), 7.
[6] N. Luhmann, *A Sociological Theory of Law* (Routledge, London, 1985), 268.
[7] Lord Mackenzie Stuart, *The European Communities and the Rule of Law* (Stevens, London, 1977), 66.

The present evidence suggests that English courts are being hampered in applying proportionality owing to the absence of an authoritative statement of statutory objectives. For example, recent litigation concerning the Merchant Shipping Act 1988 revealed that a variety of different objectives could have been pursued by the legislation.[8] In 1983 the Common Fisheries Policy introduced the allocation of national quotas to be administered by each Member State. The 1988 Act, passed following the increasing practice of "quota-hopping" by fishermen from other Member States, included nationality, domicile and residency conditions which fishermen had to fulfil in order to register a vessel and therefore fish under the British quota. The Act was challenged as an unlawful restriction of Community law rights. The discovery of documents ordered by the High Court revealed that different ministers had different views concerning the objectives pursued by the legislation. As Nicholas Green has explained, the objectives of the Act were described in a variety of different ways; sometimes the differences were subtle and at other times more profound. Furthermore, the sources in which the objectives were to be found included a wide variety of sources not immediately accessible. Sources included, among other things: instructions to parliamentary counsel; inter-departmental minutes and notes; internal briefing notes to ministers; advice from law officers to the Cabinet and ministers; correspondence between the Government and the European Commission; and letters from MPs to their constituents.[9] It is surely a matter for concern in the English legal system when a High Court judge describes reaching a decision with regard to the aims of an Act of Parliament as "a difficult task".[10]

The courts themselves have sought to compensate for the failure of Parliament by allowing reference to the reports of parliamentary proceedings in *Hansard*.[11] However, this may not, by itself, be sufficient, for the following reasons. First, this is a relatively limited development; courts may refer to *Hansard* only when the ordinary meaning of the statute is ambiguous or obscure. Secondly, statements made in Parliament with this rule in mind may reflect different positions on the same issue, which can obscure the underlying objective. Furthermore, some judges themselves are reluctant to adopt a purposive approach to statutory interpretation because, in the absence of Parliament clearly stating its objectives, a court must impose its own policy on the ordinary meaning of the statutory wording.[12]

Under the Human Rights Act 1998 the courts now have the jurisdiction to examine the compatibility of any British law against the rights and liberties guaranteed under the European Convention of Human Rights. The Act allows

---

[8] *R. v. Secretary of State for Transport, ex parte Factortame Ltd.* [1998] 3 CMLR 192, CA; [1999] 4 All ER 906, HL.

[9] N. Green, "Proportionality and the Supremacy of Parliament in the U.K." in E. Ellis (ed.), *The Principle of Proportionality in the Laws of Europe* (Hart Publishing, Oxford, 1999), 145, 162.

[10] *W.H. Smith Do It All Ltd.* v. *Peterborough City Council* [1991] 4 All ER 193, 219e, *per* Schiemann J.

[11] *Pepper* v. *Hart* [1993] AC 593.

[12] Lord Oliver, "A Judicial View of Modern Legislation" (1993) 14 *Statute LR* 1.

the courts to issue a declaration of incompatibility if they consider that an Act of Parliament infringes any of the Convention rights. In examining the proportionality of an Act against a Convention right, the court will know the ends for which Parliament was acting. In this regard the Convention eases the task placed on the court since it sets out the legitimate purposes for which the rights and liberties contained therein may be restricted. For example, Article 10(2) states that freedom of expression may be subject to such restrictions necessary in a democratic society in the interests of, among other things, national security, public safety, the prevention of disorder or crime and for the protection of health and morals. The Convention specifies the limited range of legitimate purposes for which a right may be infringed. The court will need to make some judgment as to whether the challenged Act of Parliament was or may have been enacted for one or more of those purposes.

The purpose of legislation may be self-evident or apparent. Alternatively, as in the case of the Merchant Shipping Act 1988, it may be more uncertain and opaque. Parliament may delegate wide discretionary power to a public authority or give ministers the power to make regulations without any policy guidance in the legislation itself. Despite the absence of a formulated purpose, it is evident that public authorities act in the interests of some goal or end. For example, a minister may use his powers to ban a type of food in the interests of public health, or a local authority may introduce traffic charges to reduce congestion. When a challenge is made to the exercise of such powers the court will usually be informed by the respondent of the objective being pursued. The court will then be able to proceed to the next stage and assess whether alternative means were available. If the respondent refuses to give reasons for its decision, the court should be able to require the authority to identify the purpose behind its decision, otherwise the court will effectively be precluded from undertaking the proportionality test.

Under section 6 of the Human Rights Act 1998 it is unlawful for a public authority to act in a way which is incompatible with a Convention right. Again, the court will have to determine whether the public authority's decision was or may have been made in pursuit of one or more of the legitimate purposes detailed in the Convention.

2. INSTITUTIONAL ABILITY

In their discussion of judicial review, Harlow and Rawlings point out that "[t]he judges must pay due heed to the collective, public interest in good administration.[13] In relation to proportionality, this translates into the requirement that the court should declare a measure to be unlawful only if it is certain that the

---

[13] C. Harlow and R. Rawlings, *Law and Administration* (Butterworths, London, 2nd ed. 1997), 574.

same policy result could have been achieved with equal effect through other means. Questions over the effectiveness of alternative means vary in their complexity. For example, it may appear self-evident that the revocation of a trading licence is a disproportionate penalty to impose upon a trader who is caught urinating in the street, and that a lesser penalty would have merited.[14] However, other cases will raise more complex and difficult questions of policy implementation and administrative effectiveness. The court may be required to undertake assessments as to fact, and scrutinise scientific and technical material. The court will therefore require the necessary procedural tools and knowledge. How, in this respect, might English courts manage in applying proportionality?

To ascertain whether it was factually possible for the public authority to have used a less-intrusive measure, the court will have to make findings of fact. However, the ability of English courts to perform this task will be severely limited because "[u]nder public law, it is not the role of the courts to find facts: it is not for the court to specify what is reasonable and its views on policy questions are normally of no relevance".[15] Courts shrink from engaging in fact-finding for fear of substituting their own view of the merits for that of the public authority. As has been noted, if courts are unable to probe behind the formal account of how a measure was made, their power to review will be severely limited.[16]

If courts are to integrate proportionality, they will need to reassess the dualisms implicit here. As regards proportionality, the distinction between law and fact and also that between law and policy have little, if any, meaning. In applying that principle, the court is asking whether a particular measure was the most appropriate way of achieving a policy objective. In so doing, the court will need to make assessments of fact as to whether the authority could have adopted an alternative course. At the same time, the court is also concerned with the effective implementation of public policy. To insist upon strict distinctions in this context between the legal, factual and policy assessments involved is untenable.

The European Court, as well as French and German administrative courts, recognise that proportionality requires an examination of the factual basis of decisions. From a German perspective the unwillingness of the English courts to inquire into questions of fact represents a serious shortcoming.[17] Regardless of how English judicial review compares with that of German courts, the inability to make judgments of fact will seriously prejudice English courts from applying proportionality effectively.

---

[14] *R. v. Barnsley Metropolitan Borough Council, ex parte Hook* [1976] 1 WLR 1052.

[15] H. Woolf, "Public—Private Law: Why the Divide? A Personal View" [1986] *PL* 220, 225.

[16] M. Purdue, "The Scope for Fact-Finding in Judicial Review", in G. Hand and J. McBride (eds), *Droit Sans Frontieres: Essays in Honour of L Neville Brown* (Holdsworth Club, Birmingham, 1991), 193.

[17] See, e.g., D. Conrad, "Introduction", in M.P. Singh, *German Administrative Law in Common Law Perspective* (Springer-Verlag, Berlin, 1985), xii; M. Brenner, "Administrative Judicial Protection in Europe: General Principles" (1997) 9 *European Review of Public Law* 595, 614.

The courts will also need to reassess their accepted notions of what constitutes a justiciable question of public law. Proportionality may raise some novel questions concerning the implementation of public policy which are beyond the usual questions of *vires* and unreasonableness. The difficulties faced by courts in this regard was demonstrated in the Sunday trading cases. The issue was whether restrictions on Sunday trading under the Shops Act 1950 constituted a restriction on the free movement of goods under Community law.[18] If a shop could not trade certain goods on Sunday, did this amount to an unlawful restriction on intra-Community trade? Local authorities seeking to enforce the Act against traders argued that the restrictions were justifiable as a political choice to ensure that working hours arranged in accordance with national or regional socio-cultural characteristics. The question for the English courts to determine was whether the restriction on the free movement of goods was proportionate in light of the legislative objective of protecting employees. One of the cases came before Hoffmann J., as he then was, who was asked to undertake the proportionality test, which "was, to say the least, an unusual experience for an English lawyer".[19] Hoffmann J. considered that this was an inquiry quite unsuited to the judicial process:[20]

> "In my judgment it is not my function to carry out the balancing exercise or to form my own view on whether the legislative objective could be achieved by other means. These questions involve compromises between competing interests which in a democratic society must be resolved by the legislature. The duty of the court is only to inquire whether the compromise adopted by the United Kingdom Parliament, so far as it affects Community trade, is one which a reasonable legislature could have reached. The function of the court is to review the acts of the legislature but not to substitute its own policies or values."

The task of achieving a practical balance between conflicting interests is an established feature of German and European public law.[21] As the competing values do not dictate a specific result it is necessary for the administrative court to concretise them by finding an optimal balance so that both are ensured as far as possible. This weighing exercise is necessary because competing values are worthy of being realised and ought to be upheld within the limits of what is factually possible. However, Hoffmann J. considered that the judicial role precluded any exercise in optimising conflicting interests since this would mean the court substituting its own policies. The issue was "so far from being justiciable as to be bizarre".[22] In a subsequent case before the European Court,

---

[18] See, generally, R. Rawlings, "The Eurolaw Game: Some Deductions from a Saga" (1993) 20 *JLS* 309.

[19] Lord Hoffmann, "A Sense of Proportion" (1997) 32 *Irish Jurist* 49, 55.

[20] *Stoke-on-Trent City Council* v. *B. & Q. plc* [1991] Ch. 48, 69D-E.

[21] See, e.g., J. Habermas, *Between Facts and Norms: Contributions to a Discourse Theory of Law and Democracy* (Polity Press, Cambridge, 1996), 254; W. van Gerven, "The Effect of Proportionality on the Actions of Member States of the European Community: National Viewpoints from Continental Europe", in Ellis (ed.), above at n. 10, 37, 45–6.

[22] Lord Hoffmann, "The Influence of the European Principle of Proportionality upon UK Law", in Ellis (ed.), above at n. 10, 107, 113.

Hoffmann J. was criticised by Advocate-General van Gerven for failing to provide effective protection of Community rights because he refused to undertake this weighing exercise.[23]

The significance of this case lies in the different approaches of Hoffman J. and the Advocate-General. Both agreed that the Shops Act did not breach Community law. However, whereas Hoffman J. refused to assess the proportionality of the Act, the Advocate-General was of the opinion that the judge should have performed this exercise. To apply proportionality, therefore, courts must go beyond their limited, rule-based jurisprudence and realise values in specific situations by establishing what is factually possible. As the Sunday trading cases show, proportionality may require courts to expand their conception of justiciability beyond its traditional confines.

A related issue is the relative lack of judicial knowledge and experience of governmental processes. English judges are drawn from the Bar and not from the civil service. Whereas in France and Germany, there is a close link between administrative judges and the state bureaucracy, the English judiciary view their separation from the administration as a sign of their independence. The judges receive their political education in the traditions of common law and know how to maintain the "delicate constitutional balance" between themselves, Parliament and Ministers of the Crown.[24] Judges hearing applications for judicial review are given no training in public administration and may have little or no experience of governmental processes.[25]

English judges' comparative lack of experience of governmental processes could seriously prejudice the effectiveness of any proportionality review, as judges themselves accept. Sir Thomas Bingham has intimated that in applying proportionality a judge is "beginning to enter the administrator's mind rather than simply reviewing the process by which the decision was reached".[26] In the view of Lord Scarman, the application of proportionality requires "administrative skill and experience".[27] In other words, it requires the judge to think in administrative terms; to consider how the public good can most effectively be implemented requires more knowledge and understanding of governmental processes than English judges habitually possess.

This point may be drawn out by comparing the review of economic policy measures by the European Court with that of English courts. When engaged in

[23] Case C–306/88 *Rochdale Borough Council* v. *Stewart John Anders* [1992] ECR I–6457, paras 27–31 of the Advocate-General's opinion. See also A. Arnull, "What Shall We Do on Sunday?" (1991) 16 *EL Rev.* 112.

[24] See *R.* v. *Secretary of State for the Environment, ex parte National and Local Government Officers' Association* [1993] 5 Admin. LR 785, 801B.

[25] See L. Blom-Cooper, "Lawyers and Public Administrators: Separate and Unequal" [1984] *PL* 215; G. Drewry, "Public Lawyers and Public Administrators: Prospects for an Alliance?" (1986) 64 *Public Administration* 173.

[26] T.H. Bingham, "'There is a World Elsewhere': The Changing Perspectives of English Law" (1992) 41 *ICLQ* 513, 524.

[27] Lord Scarman, in JUSTICE: Annual Members Conference, *Judicial Review of Administrative Action* (London, 30 May 1987), 17.

reviewing the proportionality of policy implementation, the European Court will invalidate the measure only if there is a manifest error. Nonetheless, it is clear that the Court will intervene if the measure imposes a particularly onerous burden.[28] English courts, on the other hand, have signalled their reluctance to intervene in this context. As Lord Bridge pointed out, the formulation and implementation of economic policy are essentially matters of political judgment and will not be susceptible to challenge except on the extremes of bad faith, improper purpose or manifest absurdity.[29] While English courts have not absolved themselves of the responsibility to ensure legality in this context, it is difficult to imagine a case where an applicant would be successful. It has been suggested that courts simply lack "both the institutional confidence and constitutional legitimacy to perform the exercise demanded of them".[30] In short, English judges feel unable to undertake a proportionality review concerning the implementation of economic policy because they lack the necessary understanding of governmental processes.

3. JUDICIAL REVIEW AND PROPORTIONALITY

Possessing a wider knowledge in relation to fact-finding and being better informed of administration are necessary but not sufficient conditions for the application of proportionality. If judges are to apply the principle effectively then the whole nature and purpose of judicial review jurisdiction must be reconsidered. Proportionality means that judges have to compare possible solutions to an administrative task. They must decide whether the measure was the most appropriate way of achieving a specific policy goal. Previously, the judiciary have eschewed this approach for fear of becoming embroiled in political disputes. If they choose to utilise proportionality, then judges will need to emphasise the democratic basis of review: public authorities decide which objectives are worthy of achievement. The court's jurisdiction would no longer be defined solely in terms of detailing what public authorities cannot do, but would extend to inquiring whether they could perform their tasks more effectively. While anxious to ensure sensitive treatment for individuals, courts would also need to accept a role in evaluating governmental performance.

In undertaking this inquiry judges would need to examine the factual and policy basis of the measure. Having identified the objective behind the decision, they would have to seek out alternative means of securing that social interest. Such alternative courses of action would then need to be compared against the challenged measure. Is the alternative course equally capable of fulfilling the

---

[28] See above at ch. 4, p. 77.

[29] *R. v. Secretary of State for the Environment, ex parte Hammersmith and Fulham London Borough Council* [1991] 1 AC 521, 597F–H, *per* Lord Bridge.

[30] M. Loughlin, *Legality and Locality: The Role of Law in Central-Local Government Relations* (Clarendon Press, Oxford, 1996), 320.

administration's policy goal? Would it impose less of a burden on private interests? If so, would the alternative measure provide an appropriate way of achieving the policy goal from the administrator's perspective? Would the adoption of the alternative measure require such a degree of administrative reorganisation and inconvenience thereby rendering itself disproportionate?

Undertaking a proportionality inquiry is by no means an easy task. There may well be various interests beyond the specific case which may be affected by the court's decision. Judges will need to be aware of the consequences of their actions and of the limitations of their own procedures and knowledge. While it cannot acquiesce in favour of the public authority, the court needs to be informed, as far as possible, of the realities of public administration. At the same time, in declaring a measure to be disproportionate, the court must be certain that an alternative course of action is available to the public authority and that it is equally effective in terms of achieving the overall objective.

Despite the changes necessary for the effective adoption of proportionality, it is unlikely that its use would result in numerous public measures being struck down as unlawful. As was seen in chapter 4 above, proportionality in European Community law operates through a variable framework of review. The European Court strikes down decisions only in relatively few cases. There are numerous factors which influence the operation of proportionality, which would also apply if it were integrated into English law, for example if the adverse impact on an individual is of a limited nature only, or if there is an urgent need for a public authority to respond to a developing situation. The real benefit of proportionality is found in the more structured process which enables the court to guide the administration on the most appropriate ways to achieve its goals.

4. CONCLUSION

This chapter has identified some of the issues relating to the adoption of proportionality in English law. It must be clear how courts should handle proportionality. The courts could employ the doctrine to examine the appropriateness and necessity of administrative action, but it is apparent that further changes are required. If they are to operate proportionality review effectively, the courts will need to be oriented towards the public functions of government, adopt a more purposive approach to statutory interpretation and develop their knowledge of governmental processes. Parliament should identify the objectives of Acts clearly by setting them out in a preamble. In addition to all this, the very nature of judicial review would need to be reassessed.

So, what of proportionality? It is highly likely that the courts will integrate this principle into English law. However, while courts may adopt this language of review, they will limit the operation of the doctrine to matters which they feel come within their competence. As Lord Scarman has intimated, it is unlikely that British judges could operate a proportionality doctrine effectively outside the field of fundamental rights.[31] Despite this limitation, the adoption of proportionality would be a welcome step in the direction of a more rational administrative law. The alternative of drawing a sharp distinction between European and non-European issues scarcely presents an attractive way forward.

---

[31] Lord Scarman, above at n. 27, 17.

6

Conclusion

THIS BOOK HAS examined the development of legitimate expectations and proportionality in English law by means of a comparison with European Community law. Only by placing the principles in the different approaches to administrative law has it been possible to make sense of the jurisprudence. English administrative law has developed within the common law tradition, which has traditionally declined to recognise special public law principles. By contrast, the Continental tradition is predicated on a conceptual division between public and private law, with special administrative courts applying distinct principles. From this tradition, legitimate expectations and proportionality evolved as norms guiding the administration in the pursuit of collective goals along the lines of purposive rationality.

In integrating the principles, English courts have experienced difficulties which the European Court of Justice has managed to avoid. English judges have been unsure of the role and purpose of the principles. They have confused and prevaricated over the meaning of legitimate expectations. They have also disagreed over whether the doctrine is a substantive as opposed to a purely procedural doctrine, and over the appropriate test to determine the legitimacy of an expectation. The judges have failed to appreciate the nature of proportionality as a way of ensuring a rational relationship between means and ends, rather than simply a review of the merits. They have also lacked the institutional confidence to undertake the assessments involved in a proportionality inquiry.

It could be argued that we should not place too much weight on the relative success of the European Court in handling the principles, when compared with English courts. After all, Community law is of comparatively recent origin and therefore more malleable than common law. The European Court is composed of judges who draw upon legal principles from their own national legal systems when developing the general principles of Community law. Furthermore, the collegiate nature of decision-making in the European Court precludes dissenting judgments. It could be argued that the incremental growth of common law is of positive value since it enables judges to express their differing views and allows the law to develop through open debate.

Despite these considerations it is evident that English law has lacked the cultural and institutional infrastructure which has characterised Continental legal systems and influenced the European Court. Although the High Court has augmented its role as a public law jurisdiction, judges have been uncertain whether to retain their traditional anti-rationalist approach or develop distinct public law principles. It has been precisely this tension, symbolised by the move from *Wednesbury* unreasonableness to the principles examined here, which has preoccupied judges and commentators.

If legitimate expectations and proportionality are to be integrated more effectively into English law, the courts must recognise their role in controlling and guiding the implementation of public policy. Public authorities are charged with the task of achieving certain functions, and make decisions on behalf of the public as a whole. While some readjustment of private interests may be required to achieve a desired policy objective, the risk of arbitrariness has increased with the expansion of state activities. The sheer complexity of public administration means that such restrictions may not be fully thought out or wholly necessary. In seeking an optimum balance between the performance of public functions and the protection of private interests, an administrative court can ensure that the interests of the individual are upheld as far as possible. After all, effective administration can be carried out only with the co-operation of the public. If public authorities are required to take account of values such as legitimate expectations and proportionality, this will improve the quality and acceptability of their decisions. It is precisely this role that courts must undertake if they are to develop distinct public law principles.

For some, the politicised nature of judicial decision-making is sufficient to justify the boundaries around it being drawn very tightly.[1] However, in modern conditions of social and administrative complexity recourse to law is inevitable in order to resolve disputes and restore social order. It is unrealistic and inadequate to rely solely upon the goodwill of public authorities to provide redress. The distinctive advantage of having a specialist administrative jurisdiction is that it can combine legal protection with an awareness of the realities and needs of public administration. Furthermore, it can lend overall coherence to the wide range of policy programmes by articulating the general norms that should inform public action. However, the difficulties of this task should not be underestimated. English courts need a greater awareness and knowledge of governmental processes than they presently possess and a wider ability to make findings of fact. Parliament and public authorities should identify their objectives clearly in law-making. In addition, it must be accepted that law can play a legitimate role in positively structuring and guiding administrative activity.

This book has highlighted the different approaches to administrative law between the common law and Continental Europe and the European Community. Nevertheless, this should not be taken to imply that convergence is to be ruled out. As Otto Kahn-Freund once remarked, all purely intellectual obstacles to assimilation are, in practice, surmountable; the real obstacles are to be found in the widely differing histories, political and social structures of

---

[1] See J.A.G. Griffith, "The Political Constitution" (1979) 42 *MLR* 1.

European countries.[2] The major intellectual obstacle to the assimilation of legitimate expectations and proportionality in English and Community law has concerned the role of law in government. If, through the integration of the principles, English law is receptive to the idea that, in the modern state, law can rationalise public action in accordance with its purposes, this will have provided a means of promoting intellectual convergence. In light of the increasing convergence of administrative programmes through the processes of European integration, overcoming this particular intellectual obstacle may be no bad thing.

[2] O. Kahn-Freund, "Common Law and Civil Law—Imaginary and Real Obstacles to Assimilation", in M. Cappelletti (ed.), *New Perspectives For a Common Law of Europe* (Sijthoff, Leyden, 1978), 137, 163–4.

Bibliography

AKEHURST, M. (1981) "The Application of General Principles of Law by the Court of Justice of the European Communities", 52 *BYIL* 29.

ALLAN, T.R.S. (1993) *Law, Liberty, and Justice: The Legal Foundations of British Constitutionalism.*

ALLEN, C.K. (1927) *Law in the Making.*

—— (1931) *Bureaucracy Triumphant.*

ALLISON, J.W.F. (1994) "The Procedural Reason for Judicial Restraint", *PL* 452.

—— (1996) *A Continental Distinction in the Common Law: A Historical and Comparative Perspective on English Public Law.*

ARENA, G. (1991) "Rights vis-à-vis the Administration: Commentary", in A. Cassese, A. Clapham and J. Weiler (eds), *Human Rights and the European Community: Methods of Protection.*

ARNULL, A. (1991) "What Shall We Do on Sunday?", 16 *EL Rev.* 112.

AVERY, G. (1984) "The Common Agricultural Policy: a Turning Point?", 21 *CML Rev.* 481.

BAGEHOT, W. (1993) *The English Constitution.*

BAKER, P.V. (1986) "Lord Diplock 1907–1985", 102 *LQR* 1.

BALDWIN, R. and HORNE, D. (1986) "Expectations in a Joyless Landscape", 49 *MLR* 685.

BARENTS, R. (1985) "The System of Deposits in Community Agricultural Law: Efficiency v Proportionality", 10 *EL Rev.* 239.

BARKER, E. (1914) "The 'Rule of Law'", 2 *Political Quarterly* 117.

BAX, C.J. (1992) "Judicial Control of the Administration in the Netherlands", 4 *European Review of Public Law* 71.

BELL, J. (1991) "Reflections on the Procedure of the Conseil d'État", in G. Hand and J. McBride (eds), *Droit Sans Frontiers: Essays in Honour of L. Neville Brown* .

—— (1991/2) "The English Lawyer in the Europe of 1993", 34 *University of Leeds Review* 181.

—— (1998) "Mechanisms for Cross-fertilisation of Administrative Law in Europe", in J. Beatson and T. Tridimas (eds), *New Directions in European Public Law.*

BINGHAM, SIR THOMAS (1992) " 'There is a World Elsewhere': The Changing Perspectives of English Law", 41 *ICLQ* 513.

BLANKENAGEL, A. (1992) "The Concept of Subjective Rights as the Focal Point of German Administrative Law", 11 *Tel Aviv University Studies in Law* 79.

BLOM-COOPER, L. and DREWRY, G. (1972) *Final Appeal: A Study of the House of Lords in its Judicial Capacity.*

—— (1984) "Lawyers and Public Administrators: Separate and Unequal", *PL* 215.

BORCHARDT, K.-D. (1988) "*Vertrauensschutz im Europäischen Gemeinschaftsrecht: Die Rechtsprechung des EuGH von Algera über CNTA bis Mulder und von Deetzen*", 15 *Europäische Grundrechte Zeitschrift* 309.

BOYRON, S. (1992) "Proportionality in English Administrative Law: A Faulty Translation?", 12 *OJLS* 237.

BREDIMAS, A. (1978) "Comparative Law in the Court of Justice of the European Communities", in *The Yearbook of World Affairs 1978 Volume 32.*

BRENNER, M. (1997) "Administrative Judicial Protection in Europe: General Principles", 9 *European Review of Public Law* 595.

BURKE, E. (1982) *Reflections on the Revolution in France.*

BUTLER, G.G. (1957) *The Tory Tradition: Bolingbroke, Burke, Disraeli, Salisbury.*

CANE, P. (1996) *An Introduction to Administrative Law.*

CANNAN, E. (1912) *The History of Local Rates in England.*

CARDWELL, M. (1996) *Milk Quotas: European Community and United Kingdom Law.*

CARNWATH, SIR ROBERT (1996) "The Reasonable Limits of Local Authority Powers", *PL* 244.

CASSESE, S. (1990) "Towards a European Model of Public Administration", in D.S. Clark (ed.), *Comparative and Private International Law: Essays in Honour of John Henry Merryman on his Seventieth Birthday.*

CHITI, M.P. (1992) "Administrative Comparative Law", 4 *European Review of Public Law* 11.

COKE, C.J. SIR EDWARD (1738) *The Third Part of the Reports of Edward Coke.*

COLLINI, S. (1991) *Public Moralists: Political Thought and Intellectual Life in Britain 1850–1930.*

Councils of State and the Supreme Courts of Justice of the Member States of the European Communities (1976) *Discretionary Power and the Advisability of Administrative Decisions; The Extent and Limitations of Judicial Control.*

Councils of State and the Supreme Courts of Justice of Member States of the European Community (1980) *The Power of the Courts—both Superior and Inferior Courts and Bodies Exercising Quasi-Judicial Functions—to Award Damages in Administrative Actions.*

CRAIG, P.P. (1992) "Legitimate Expectations: A Conceptual Analysis", 108 *LQR* 79.

—— (1994) "Proportionality: Lessons from Community Law", *The European Advocate* 2.

—— (1996) "Substantive Legitimate Expectations in Domestic and Community Law", 55 *CLJ* 289.

—— (1997) "Substantive Legitimate Expectations and the Principles of Judicial Review", in *The Common Law of Europe and the Public Law of the United Kingdom.*

—— (1999) "Unreasonableness and Proportionality in UK Law", in Ellis, E. (ed.), *The Principle of Proportionality in the Laws of Europe.*

—— (1999) *Administrative Law.*

—— and DE BURCA, G. (1998) *EU Law: Text, Cases and Materials.*

DAINTITH, T. (ed.) (1995) *Implementing EC Law in the United Kingdom: Structures For Indirect Rule.*

DAVIS, K.C. (1961) "The Future of Judge-Made Public Law in England: A Problem of Practical Jurisprudence", 61 *Columbia LR* 201.

DE BÚRCA, G. (1993) "The Principle of Proportionality and its Application in EC Law", 13 *Yearbook of European Law* 105.

—— (1997) "Proportionality and *Wednesbury* Unreasonableness: The Influence of Legal Concepts on UK Law", 3 *EPL* 561.

DE SMITH, S.A., WOOLF, H. and JOWELL, J. (1995) *Judicial Review of Administrative Action.*

DEHOUSSE, R. (1998) *The European Court of Justice.*

DENNING, SIR ALFRED (1949) *Freedom Under the Law*.

DEVLIN, P. (1956) "The Common Law, Public Policy and the Executive", 9 *CLP* 1.

DICEY, A.V. (1905) *Lectures on the Relationship Between Law and Public Opinion in England during the Nineteenth Century*.

—— (1959) *An Introduction to the Study of the Law of the Constitution*.

DICKSON, B. (1989) "The Contribution of Lord Diplock to the General Law of Contract", 9 *OJLS* 441.

DIPLOCK, SIR KENNETH (1965) *The Courts as Legislators*.

—— (1969) "Preface", in J.F. Garner and A.R. Galbraith (eds), *Judicial Control of the Administrative Process*.

—— (1971) "Judicial Control of Administrative Action", 24 *CLP* 1.

—— (1972) "Foreword", in B. Schwartz and H.W.R. Wade, *Legal Control of Government*.

—— (1972) "The Common Market and the Common Law", 6 *The Law Teacher* 3.

—— (1974) "Administrative Law: Judicial Review Reviewed", 33 *CLJ* 233.

—— (1978) "Judicial Development of Law in the Commonwealth", in *Proceedings and Papers of the Fifth Commonwealth Law Conference*.

DONALDSON, A.G. (1991) "The High Priests of the Mystery: A Note on Two Centuries of Parliamentary Draftsmen", in W. Finnie, C.M.G. Himsworth and N. Walker (eds), *Edinburgh Essays in Public Law*.

DREWRY, G. (1986) "Public Lawyers and Public Administrators: Prospects for an Alliance?", 64 *Public Administration* 173.

DUBOUIS, L. (1996) *"Le droit communautaire a-t-il un impact sur la définition du droit administratif?"*, *Actualité Juridique: Droit Administratif* 102.

DUGUIT, L. (1917/18) "The Law and the State", 31 *Harvard LR* 1.

—— (1921) *Law in the Modern State*.

DUMON, F. (1976) "The Case-Law of the Court of Justice—A Critical Examination of the Methods of Interpretation", in *Judicial and Academic Conference 27–28 September 1976*.

DWORKIN, R. (1977) *Taking Rights Seriously*.

—— (1986) *Law's Empire*.

DYSON, K.H.F. (1980) *The State Tradition in Western Europe: A Study of an Idea and Institution*.

EDWARD, D. (1993) "Proportionality and Legitimate Expectations", a talk given at the Judicial Studies Board, 8 January.

ELIAS, P. (1988) "Legitimate Expectations and Judicial Review", in J. Jowell and D. Oliver (eds), *New Directions in Judicial Review*.

EMILIOU, N. (1996) *The Principle of Proportionality in European Law: A Comparative Study* .

ERRERA, R. (1985) "Dicey and French Administrative Law: A Missed Encounter?", *PL* 695.

FELDMAN, D. (1988) "Judicial Review: A Way of Controlling Government?", 66 *Public Administration* 21.

FORSYTH, C.F. (1988) "The Provenance and Protection of Legitimate Expectations", 47 *CLJ* 238.

—— (1997) *"Wednesbury* Protection of Substantive Legitimate Expectations", *PL* 375.

FRANKENBERG, G. (1998) "Remarks on the Philosophy and Politics of Public Law", 18 *LS* 177.

GALMOT, Y. (1990) *"Réflexions sur le recourse au droit comparé par la Cour de Justice des Communautés européenes"*, 6 *Revue française droit administratif* 255.

GANZ, G. (1986) "Legitimate Expectation: A Confusion of Concepts", in C. Harlow (ed.), *Public Law and Politics*.

GARNER, J.F. (1978) "The Principle of Proportionality", in *UK National Reports Submitted to the Xth International Congress on Comparative Law*.

GEERTZ, C. (1993) *The Interpretation of Cultures*.

GOFF OF CHIEVELEY, LORD (1997) "The Future of the Common Law"46 *ICLQ* 745.

GOLLER, B. and SCHMIDT, A. (1998) "Reform of the German Administrative Courts Act", 4 *EPL* 31.

GORMLEY, W.P. (1963) "The Significant Role of French Administrative Jurisprudence as Presently Applied by the Court of European Communities, With Emphasis on the Administrative Law Remedies Available to Private Litigants", 8 *South Dakota LR* 32.

GÖTZ, V. (1991) "Legislative and Executive Power under the Constitutional Requirements Entailed in the Principle of the Rule of Law", in C. Starck (ed.), *New Challenges to the German Basic Law*.

GREENE, LORD (1938) *The Judicial Office*.

—— (1944) "Law and Progress", 94 *The Law Journal* 349.

GREEN, N. (1999) "Proportionality and the Supremacy of Parliament", in Ellis, E. (ed.), *The Principle of Proportionality in the Laws of Europe*.

GRIFFITH, J.A.G. (1978) *Administrative Law and the Judges*.

—— (1979) "The Political Constitution", 42 *MLR* 1.

—— (1983) "Constitutional and Administrative Law", in P. Archer and A. Martin (eds), *More Law Reform Now: A Collection of Essays on Law Reform*.

—— (1993) *Judicial Politics Since 1920: A Chronicle*.

HABERMAS, J. (1996) *Between Facts and Norms: Contributions to a Discourse Theory of Law and Democracy*.

HADFIELD, B. (1988) "Judicial Review and the Concept of Legitimate Expectations", 39 *NILQ* 103.

HAILSHAM, LORD (1978) *The Dilemma of Democracy: Diagnosis and Prescription*.

HAMSON, C.J. (1954) *Executive Discretion and Judicial Control: An Aspect of the French Conseil d'État*.

HARLOW, C. (1994) "Changing the Mindset: The Place of Theory in English Administrative Law", 14 *OJLS* 419.

—— (1997) "Back to Basics: Reinventing Administrative Law", *PL* 245.

—— and RAWLINGS, R. (1998) *Law and Administration*.

—— (1999) "European Administrative Law and the Global Challenge", in P.P. Craig and G. de Búrca, *The Evolution of EU Law*.

HAYEK, F.A. (1960) *The Constitution of Liberty*.

—— (1973) *Law, Legislation and Liberty: A new statement of the liberal principles of justice and political economy. Volume 1: Rules and Order*.

—— (1976) *Volume 2: The Mirage of Social Justice*.

—— (1979) *Volume 3: The Political Order of a Free People*.

HEWART OF BURY, LORD (1929) *The New Despotism*.

HEUKELS, T. and MACDONNELL, A. (eds), (1997) *The Action for Damages in Community Law*.

HILL, C. (1980) *The Century of Revolution 1603–1714*.

HOBBES, T. (1996) *Leviathan*.

HOFFMANN, LORD (1997) "A Sense of Proportion", 32 *Irish Jurist* 49.

—— (1999) "The Influence of the European Principle of Proportionality upon UK Law", in Ellis, E. (ed.), *The Principle of Proportionality in the Laws of Europe.*

House of Lords European Communities Committee (1974–75) *Special Report, HL* 38.

HUBEAU, F. (1983) "*Le principe de la protection de la confiance legitime dans la jurisprudence de la cour de justice des communautes europeennes*", 19 *Cahiers de Droit Européen* 143.

HUNT, A. (1997) "Regulation of Telecommunications: the Developing EU Regulatory Framework and its Impact on the United Kingdom", 3 *EPL* 93.

HUNT, M. (1997) *Using Human Rights Law in English Courts.*

HUTTON, W. (1996) *The State We're In.*

IRVINE OF LAIRG Q.C., LORD (1996) "Judges and Decision-Makers: The Theory and Practice of *Wednesbury* Review", *PL* 59.

—— (1999) "Recent Developments in Public Law in the United Kingdom".

JACOB, J.M. (1996) *The Republican Crown: Lawyers and the Making of the State in Twentieth Century Britain.*

JACOBS, F. (1990) "The Uses of Comparative Law in the Law of the European Communities", in R. Plender (ed.), *Legal History and Comparative Law: Essays in Honour of Albert Kiralfy.*

—— (1999) "Public Law—The Impact of Europe", *PL* 232.

—— (1999) "Recent Developments in the Principle of Proportionality in European Community Law", in Ellis, E. (ed.), *The Principle of Proportionality in the Laws of Europe.*

JAFFE, L.L. and HENDERSON, E.G. (1956) "Judicial Review and the Rule of Law", 72 *LQR* 345.

JAKOB, T. (1990) "The rule of law", in C.-C. Schweitzer and D. Karsten (eds), *The Federal Republic of Germany and EC Membership Evaluated.*

JAMES, S. (1996) "The Political and Administrative Consequences of Judicial Review", 74 *Public Administration* 613.

JENNINGS, W.I. (1932) "The Report on Ministers' Powers", 10 *Public Administration* 333.

—— (1933) *The Law and the Constitution.*

—— (1935) "In Praise of Dicey 1885–1935", 13 *Public Administration* 123.

—— (1936) "Courts and Administrative Law—The Experience of English Housing Law Legislation", 49 *Harvard LR* 426.

JOHNSON, N. (1978) "Law as the Articulation of the State in Western Germany: A German tradition seen from a British Perspective", 1 *Western European Politics* 177.

JONES, H.S. (1993) *The French State in Question: Public Law and Political Argument in the Third Republic.*

JOWELL, J. and LESTER, A. (1987) "Beyond *Wednesbury:* Substantive Principles of Administrative Law", *PL* 368.

—— (1988) "Proportionality: Neither Novel Nor Dangerous", in J. Jowell and D. Oliver (eds), *New Directions in Judicial Review.*

—— (1996) "Is Proportionality an Alien Concept?", 2 *EPL* 401.

—— (1997) "Restraining the State: Politics, Principle and Judicial Review", 50 *CLP* 189.

—— (1999) "Of *Vires* and Vacuums: The Constitutional Context of Judicial Review", *PL* 448.

JUSTICE (1987) *Judicial Review of Administrative Action.*

KAHN-FREUND, O. (1974) "On Uses and Misuses of Comparative Law", 37 *MLR* 1.

KAHN-FREUND, O. (1978) "Common Law and Civil Law—Imaginary and Real Obstacles to Assimilation", in M. Cappelletti (ed.), *New Perspectives For a Common Law of Europe.*

KEETON, G.W. (1949) "The Twilight of the Common Law", *The Nineteenth Century and After* 230.

KERRY, M. (1986) "Administrative Law and Judicial Review—The Practical Effects of Developments Over the Last 25 Years in Administration in Central Government", 64 *Public Administration* 163.

KOOPMANS, T. (1991) "The Birth of European Law at the Crossroads of Legal Traditions", 39 *American Journal of Comparative Law* 493.

—— (1991) "European Public Law: Reality and Prospects", *PL* 53.

KRYGIER, M. (1986) "Law as Tradition", 5 *Law and Philosophy* 237.

KUTSCHER, H. (1976) "Methods of Interpretation as Seen by a Judge at the Court of Justice", in *Judicial and Academic Conference 27–28 September 1976.*

LAMOUREUX, F. (1983) "The Retroactivity of Community Acts in the Case Law of the Court of Justice", 20 *CML Rev.* 269.

LASKI, H.J. (1926) "Judicial Review of Social Policy in England", 39 *Harvard LR* 832

LAW COMMISSION (1993) Consultation Paper No. 126, *Administrative Law: Judicial Review and Statutory Appeals.*

LAWS, SIR JOHN (1993) "Is the High Court the Guardian of Fundamental Constitutional Rights?", *PL* 59.

—— (1994) "English and Community Law: Uniformity of Principle", *The European Advocate.*

—— (1996) "The Constitution: Morals and Rights", *PL* 622.

—— (1998) "The Constitutional Foundations of Modern Public Law", 10 *European Review of Public Law* 579.

—— (1998) "*Wednesbury*", in C. Forsyth and I. Hare (eds), *The Golden Metwand and the Crooked Cord: Essays on Public Law in Honour of Sir William Wade QC.*

LETOURNER, M. (1973) "The Concept of Equity in French Public Law", in R.A. Newman (ed.), *Equity in the World's Legal Systems: A Comparative Study.*

LOCKE, J. (1993) *Two Treatises of Government.*

LORENZ, W. (1964) "General Principles of Law: Their Elaboration in the Court of Justice of the European Communities", 13 *American Journal of Comparative Law* 1.

LOUGHLIN, M. (1991) "Sitting on a Fence at Carter Bar: In Praise of J.D.B. Mitchell", 36 *Juridical Review* 135.

—— (1992) *Public Law and Political Theory.*

—— (1996) *Legality and Locality: The Role of Law in Central-Local Government Relations.*

—— (2000) *Sword and Scales: An Examination of the Relationship between Law and Politics.*

LUHMANN, N. (1979) "Trust: a mechanism for the reduction of social complexity", in *Trust and Power: Two Works by Niklas Luhmann.*

—— (1985) *A Sociological Theory of Law.*

MACKENZIE STUART, LORD (1977) *The European Communities and the Rule of Law.*

—— (1983) "Legitimate Expectations and Estoppel in Community Law and English Administrative Law", *Legal Issues of European Integration* 53.

—— (1986) "Control of Power Within the European Communities", 11 *Holdsworth LR* 1.

—— (1987) "Recent Developments in English Administrative Law—The Impact of

Europe?", in F. Capotorti (ed.), *Du droit international au droit de l'integration: Liber Amicorum Pierre Pescatore*.

MAINE, SIR HENRY (1883) *Dissertations on Early Law and Custom*.

MAITLAND, F.W. (1911) "Why the History of English Law is not Written", in H.A.L. Fisher (ed.), *The Collected Papers of Frederic William Maitland Volume 1*.

MANCINI, G.F. and KEELING, D.T. (1994) "Democracy and the European Court of Justice", 57 *MLR* 175.

MARQUAND, D. (1988) *The Unprincipled Society: New Demands and Old Politics*.

MARR, A. (1996) *Ruling Britannia: The Failure and Future of British Democracy*.

MÉNY, Y., MULLER, P. and QUERMONNE, J.-L. (1996) *Adjusting to Europe: the impact of the European Union on national institutions and policies*.

MERTENS DE WILMARS, J. (1983) "The Case-Law of the Court of Justice in Relation to the Review of the Legality of Economic Policy in Mixed-Economy Systems", *Legal Issues of European Integration* 1.

MESTRE, A. (1974) *Le Conseil d'État: Proteurs des Privileges de l'Administration*.

MILL, J.S. (1987) "Bentham", in J.S. Mill and J. Bentham, *Utilitarianism and Other Essays*.

MISZTAL, B.A. (1996) *Trust in Modern Societies: The Search for the Bases of Social Order*.

MITCHELL, J.D.B. (1995) "The Causes and Effects of the Absence of a System of Public Law in the United Kingdom", *PL* 94.

—— (1968) *Constitutional Law*.

—— (1969) "Why European Institutions?", in L.J. Brinkhorst and J.D.B. Mitchell, *European Law and Institutions*.

—— (1976) "Administrative Law and Policy Effectiveness", in J.A.G. Griffith (ed.), *From Policy to Administration: Essays in Honour of William A. Robson*.

—— (1978) "Law, Democracy and Political Institutions", in M. Cappelletti (ed.), *New Perspectives For a Common Law of Europe*.

—— (1979) "The Sovereignty of Parliament and Community Law: The Stumbling-Block That Isn't There", 55 *International Affairs* 33.

—— (1980) "What Happened to the Constitution on 1st January 1973?", 11 *Cambrian LR* 69.

MOWBRAY, A.R. (1985) "Administrative Guidance and Judicial Review", *PL* 558.

—— (1990) "A Right to Official Advice: The Parliamentary Commissioner's Perspective", *PL* 68.

NEVILLE BROWN, L. and BELL, J.S. with the assistance of Galabert, J.-M. (1998) *French Administrative Law*.

NEWARK, F.H. (1955) Book Review, 71 *LQR* 571.

OAKESHOTT, M. (1962) *Rationalism in Politics and other essays*.

—— (1975) *On Human Conduct*.

—— (1983) *On History and other essays*.

NOLTE, G. (1994) "General Principles of German and European Administrative Law—A Comparison in Historical Perspective", 57 *MLR* 191.

OLIVER, LORD (1993) "A Judicial View of Modern Legislation", 14 *Statute LR* 1.

OSSENBÜHL, F. (1972) "*Vertrauensschutz im sozialen Rechtsstaat*", 25 *Die Öffentliche Verwaltung* 25.

OULTON, D. (1997) "How Widely Accepted as a General Principle is Proportionality?", 12 *Commonwealth Judicial Journal* 17.

PAINE, T. (1984) *Rights of Man*.

PAKUSCHER, E.K. (1976–77) "The Use of Discretion in German Law", 44 *University of Chicago LR* 94.

PARKER OF WADDINGTON, LORD (1959) *Recent Developments in the Supervisory Powers of the Courts Over Inferior Tribunals*.

PESCATORE, P. (1980) *"Le Recourse, dans la Jurisprudence de la Cour de Justice des Communautés Européennes, a des Normes Déduites de la Comparison des Droits des États Membres"*, 32 *Revue Internationale de Droit Comparé* 337.

POCOCK, J.G.A. (1987) *The Ancient Constitution and the Feudal Law: A Study of English Historical Thought in the Seventeenth Century*.

PORT, F.J. (1929) *Administrative Law*.

PURDUE, M. (1991) "The Scope of Fact-Finding in Judicial Review", in G. Hand and J. McBride (eds), *Droit Sans Frontieres: Essays in Honour of L. Neville Brown*.

QUESTIAUX, N. (1995) "Administration and the Rule of Law: The Preventative Role of the French Conseil d'État", *PL* 247.

RÄDLER, P. (1992) "Judicial Protection Against the Executive by German Administrative Courts", *Admin. Review* 78.

RAWLINGS, R. (1993) "The Eurolaw Game: Some Deductions from a Saga", 20 *JLS* 309.

RAWLS, J. (1972) *A Theory of Justice*.

RAZ, J. (1979) *The Authority of Law: Essays on Law and Morality*.

REDLICH, J. and HIRST, F.W. (1903) *Local Government in England*.

REICH, N. (1996) "Judge-made 'Europe à la carte': Some Remarks on Recent Conflicts between European and German Constitutional Law Provoked by the Banana Litigation", 7 *European Journal of International Law* 103.

Report of the Committee on Ministers' Powers Report (1932) Cmd 4060.

RIVERO, J. (1978) *"Vers un Droit Commun Européen: Nouvelles Perspectives en Droit Administratif"*, in M. Cappelletti (ed.), *New Perspectives For a Common Law of Europe*.

ROBSON, W.A. (1948) *Public Administration Today*.

—— (1951) *Justice and Administrative Law: A Study of the British Constitution*.

—— (1979) *"Justice and Administrative Law* Reconsidered", 32 *CLP* 107.

SCARMAN, SIR LESLIE (1972) "Law and Administration: A Change in Relationship", 50 *Public Administration* 253.

—— (1990) "The Development of Administrative Law: Obstacles and Opportunities", *PL* 490.

SCHEUNER, U. (1963) *"Der Einfluß des französischen Verwaltungsrechts auf die deutsche Rechtsentwicklung"*, 16 *Die Öffentliche Verwaltung* 714.

SCHMIDT-AßMANN, E. (1993) "Basic Principles of German Administrative Law", 35 *Journal of the Indian Law Institute* 65.

SCHUPPERT, G.F. (1995) "On the Evolution of a European State: Reflections on the Conditions of and Prospects for a European Constitution", in J.J. Hesse and N. Johnson (eds), *Constitutional Policy and Change in Europe*.

SCHWARTZ, B. (1954) *French Administrative Law and the Common-Law World*.

SCHWARZE, J. (1992) *European Administrative Law*.

—— (1996) (ed.), *Administrative Law Under European Influence: On the convergence of the administrative laws of the EU Member States*.

SEDLEY, S. (1994) "The Sound of Silence: Constitutional Law Without a Constitution", 110 *LQR* 270.

—— (1994) "Governments, Constitutions and Judges", in G. Richardson and H. Genn (eds), *Administrative Law and Government Action: The Courts and Alternative Mechanisms of Review*.

—— (1997) "The Common Law and the Constitution", *London Review of Books*, 8 May, 8.

SHARPSTON, E. (1990) "European Community Law and the Doctrine of Legitimate Expectations: How Legitimate, and For Whom?", 11 *Northwestern Journal of International Law and Business* 87.

—— (1990) "Legitimate Expectations and Economic Reality", 15 *EL Rev.* 103.

SINGH, M.P. (1985) *German Administrative Law in Common Law Perspective*.

SINGH, R. (1994) "Making Legitimate Use of Legitimate Expectation", 144 *NLJ* 1215.

SLYNN, SIR GORDON (1987) "But in England there is no . . . ", in W. Fuerst (ed.), *Festschrift für Wolfgang Zeidler Volume 1*.

—— (1993) "Looking at European Community Texts", 14 *Statute LR* 12.

—— (1993) "European Law and the National Judge", in *Butterworth Lectures 1991–92*.

SMITH, J.A.C. (1980) "Legislative Drafting: England and Continental", 2 *Statute LR* 14.

SNYDER, F. (1985) *Law of the Common Agricultural Policy*.

—— (1993) "The Effectiveness of European Community Law: Institutions, Processes, Tools and Techniques", 56 *MLR* 19.

STEVENS, R. (1979) *Law and Politics: the House of Lords as a Judicial Body, 1800–1976*.

STURGESS, G. and CHUBB, P. (eds) (1988) *Judging the World: Law and Politics in the World's Leading Courts*.

SZLADITS, C. (1972) "The Civil Law System", in *International Encyclopedia of Comparative Law, II–2 Structure and the Divisions of the Law*.

TAY, A.E. and KAMENKA, E. (1983) "Public Law—Private Law", in S.I. Benn and G.F. Gaus (eds), *Public and Private in Social Life*.

TEUBNER, G. (ed.) (1985) *Dilemmas of Law in the Welfare State*.

—— (1998) "Legal Irritants: Good Faith in British Law or How Unifying Law Ends Up in New Divergences", 61 *MLR* 11.

TEMPLE LANG, J. (1989) "The Constitutional Principles Governing Community Legislation", 40 *NILQ* 227.

—— (1991) "The Sphere in Which Member States are Obliged to Comply with the General Principles of Law and Community Fundamental Rights Principles", *Legal Issues of European Integration* 23.

TRIDIMAS, T. (1999) "Proportionality in Community Law: Searching for the Appropriate Standard of Scrutiny", in Ellis, E. (ed.), *The Principle of Proportionality in the Laws of Europe*.

USHER, J.A. (1979) "Agricultural Markets: Their Price-Systems and Financial Mechanisms", 4 *EL Rev.* 147.

—— (1998) *General Principles of EC Law*.

VAN CAENEGEM, R.C. (1991) "The 'Rechtsstaat' in Historical Perspective", in *Legal History: A European Perspective*.

VAN GERVEN, W. (1995) "Bridging the Gap Between Community and National Laws: Towards a Principle of Homogeneity in the Field of Legal Remedies?", 32 *CML Rev.* 679.

VAN GERVEN, W. (1999) "The Effect of Proportionality on the Actions of Member States of the European Community: National Viewpoints from Continental Europe", in Ellis, E. (ed.), *The Principle of Proportionality in the Laws of Europe*.

WADE, H.W.R. (1949) "'Quasi-judicial' and its Background", 10 *CLJ* 216.

—— (1951) "The Twilight of Natural Justice?", 67 *LQR* 103.

—— (1962) "Law, Opinion and Administration", 78 *LQR* 188.

—— and FORSYTH, C.F. (1994) *Administrative Law*.

—— (1989) *Constitutional Fundamentals*.

WILBERFORCE, LORD (1986) "Lord Diplock and Administrative Law", *PL* 6.

WILLIS, J. (1933) *The Parliamentary Powers of Government Departments*.

—— (1935) "Three Approaches to Administrative Law: the Judicial, the Conceptual and the Functional", 1 *University of Toronto LJ* 53.

WOOLF, SIR HARRY (1986) "Public Law—Private Law: Why the Divide? A Personal View", *PL* 220.

—— (1992) "Judicial Review: A Possible Programme For Reform", *PL* 221.

—— (1995) "*Droit Public*—English Style", *PL* 57.

WYATT, D. (1994) "European Community Law and Public Law in the United Kingdom", in B.S. Markesinis (ed.), *The Gradual Convergence: Foreign ideas, Foreign Influences and English Law on the Eve of the 21st Century*.

Index